EVEN THE DARKNESS...

EVEN
THE
DARKNESS...

Carole Simpson

OM Publishing
PO Box 48, Bromley, Kent, England

Photo acknowledgement: Richard Summersby, FRPS.

British Library Cataloguing in Publication Data

Simpson, Carole
    Even the darkness.
    1.   Christianity
    I.   Title
    248.24092

    ISBN 1 85078 091 9

OM Publishing is an imprint of Send The Light
(Operation Mobilisation),
PO Box 48, Bromley, Kent,
BR1 3JH, England.

Production and Printing in England by
Nuprint Ltd, Station Road, Harpenden, Herts, AL5 4SE.

Note

Certain names have been changed in this book to protect the people concerned. Otherwise the events recounted are, to the best of the author's recollection, as they occurred.

Acknowledgements

I would like to say a special 'thank you' to the following people: *Christine Orme*, who edited the manuscript, for her invaluable help and advice; *Joy Nye*, for giving up valuable time to type the manuscript; my dear friend *Jane*, for all her support and encouragement during the writing of the book; *Luke* and *Charis*, for being such brilliant little children when it must have, at times, seemed like I would never finish writing.

Most of all, I would like to say 'thank you' to *Mike*, for his help, patience and great understanding—if it had not been for him I would probably never have written this book.

Foreword

This book will challenge and uplift you as you enter the world of Carole Simpson and witness the remarkable power of Christ to rebuild a broken life and to replace despair and heartache with security and fulfilment.

With honesty and humour Carole tells of her violent, deprived childhood and subsequent heroin addiction, crisis pregnancies, petty crime, and involvement in the occult.

Her precarious existence was accompanied by the trauma of three 'crisis pregnancies' and the heart-rending choice between abortion and adoption faced by so many young women today. Yet throughout that time God's light was beginning to shine into her darkness, despite constant set-backs and struggles.

I whole-heartedly commend this book as a real tonic to your faith and an important insight for our understanding and compassion. I salute those people, especially her husband Mike, who supported Carole and showed her the love of Christ.

In these times of reassessment of the role of the family in society, Carole's moving story is living proof of the need that each of us has for families who love us and care for us, whatever our standard of living or financial status. To those who are struggling, because of childhood experiences, with the concept of God as a loving Father, it also offers tremendous encouragement.

Once you have read this book—and it will not be easy to put down until you have finished—I would encourage you to pass it on to someone whom you think it would help. There are tens of thousands of 'Caroles' in our society today who have no real experience of love and hope, and it is my prayer that some of these precious forgotten ones will find what Carole Simpson found before the darkness overcomes them.

Lyndon Bowring
Executive Chairman
CARE

1

My father lay on the sofa. I stood in the doorway watching him. I hated him so much. Mum had gone to phone the doctor and my younger brother and sister had been sent to play upstairs. For as long as I could remember, my father had been someone to fear, and even now he terrified me. Cautiously I moved a little closer. His grey-tinged face was white, his eyes were closed, and his brow wore a look of concentrated pain. As he held his hand to his mouth I saw beads of perspiration on his upper lip and nose.

'Does your mouth hurt, Dad?'

'No, my chest hurts!'

I could only just hear what he'd said, and I didn't understand myself; why, when I hated him so much, was there something within me that wanted to reach out and touch or comfort him? I felt I just had to do something. My hand moved tentatively towards him. Suddenly his eyes opened and he was glaring at me.

'Tell those stupid kids to shut up!'

The moment had gone. I never saw him again.

The day of the funeral arrived. The vicar stood in the pulpit, speaking words that seemed somehow completely unconnected with my dad. As far as I knew he'd only ever been to church twice—for our christenings and for this, his funeral. He could hardly have been more irreligious.

The meaningless words came to an end, and as the organist played *Abide with Me*, I stood looking at the coffin and wondered where my father was. I remember thinking that if there were a hell that was where he would go, and the thought brought tears to my eyes. I wondered vaguely if that were where I would go too, since I had spent so many nights hating him and willing him to die.

The few of us present followed the coffin down the path, across the road and into the graveyard. Four men whose faces looked as if they were made of plastic lowered the coffin into the ground. It was a grey day, with a slight drizzle, and the ground felt soft and lumpy under my feet. Everybody filed past the grave, led by Mum.

She had been up early that morning making sandwiches for the family gathering at home after the funeral. They sat in a circle in the living-room, all dressed in black. The Hedges clan hadn't been together like this for years; some of them had hated Dad when he was alive, yet here they were drinking sherry and eating sandwiches as if they were at a picnic! This made me really angry, and yet I felt confused—after all, I hated him myself so what right had I to be angry with these people?

I told Mum I had to get out, and ran up the road to the little chapel I passed every morning on the way to school. The rain had stopped, and I sat in the porch. I needed somebody to talk to, but there was no one. My mind was in a whirl, and I found myself thinking about everything that had happened in my life up to that point ...

We had lived in three or four different places in Gloucestershire, none of them particularly special; we were always very poor. One of my earliest memories is of Dad bringing home to the caravan where we then lived a chicken he had 'found'. Mum plucked it and put it in the oven, but the police arrived while it was cooking and found the feathers in the bin; Dad was charged with theft and the chicken was produced in court as evidence—six weeks later!

Some time after this we lived in a house at Kempsford. It was in a dreadful state—in fact they knocked it down when we left there. Two rooms including the kitchen were below ground level and horribly damp, and another had to be kept locked because the floor was rotten. Water came from a pump in the garden and, there being no bathroom, we had to make do with a tin bath and an outside toilet, situated behind a huge privet hedge. As there was no cesspit the toilet had to be emptied weekly into the garden. Fortunately it was a large garden! From this toilet Mum emerged one day, holding the garden fork at arm's length in restrained triumph, with a wiggling rat on the end of it! She proceeded to drown the offending rodent in a large tub of icy water, leaving it there for at least a day to make sure it was really dead.

These incidents seem amusing now, but in reality, life was hard. My father was very jealous and extremely possessive, to the point of violence, and his anger was generally out of all proportion to the incident that aroused it. Once for instance my mother forgot to put salt in the potatoes; my father simply picked up his plate and mashed the potatoes into her hair.

My childhood was punctuated by my mother leaving home at intervals, whenever my father's violence towards her became intolerable. Once the local paper even carried a photo of us, with a plea for her to return. I never resented her leaving, but it must have added to my general sense of insecurity.

When Mum left, my father made no attempt to look after us himself in her absence. His method of coping with the situation was to pile us all in the car, and dump us with a relative, Aunty Hilda for instance; she was landed with us kids more than once.

Aunty Hilda's establishment had to be seen to be believed! She and Sam, her husband, had about nine children, whom they brought up in a medium-sized house lacking electricity; it always seemed a dark and frightening house to me. Food was cooked on a fire in the living-room, and I remember drinking tea made with condensed milk, into which we dipped bread and margarine. As might be imagined, sleeping arrangements at Aunty Hilda's were also pretty basic: my brother and I shared a bed with two others, sleeping head to toe in a room that was never warm.

Uncle Sam smoked constantly, despite the fact that he was dying of cancer. I was terrified of him; to my childish eyes he seemed very tall and gaunt, and always had a frightening asthmatic wheeze. One day, to my astonishment, he gave me threepence of his 'baccy money'; to be given something like that was a very unusual event, and I ran off clutching the money before he changed his mind!

As I sat in the chapel porch all this came back to me clearly, as if I were watching a film. In fact for much of my childhood I felt exactly like that: as though I were an onlooker, not a participant; things that happened, over which I had no control, just passed me by. It was as if, even then, I didn't let myself feel anything in case it hurt too much, as if I'd put up some invisible barrier around myself as a defence.

Of course I couldn't have put that into words, and some emotions did break through the barrier, especially where my mother was involved. I can still remember the surge of joy I felt once when my father arrived to take us home from Aunty Hilda's, because Mum had come back. When we reached home she was sitting on the lawn in a floppy sun-hat shelling peas into a colander. I was about five and I ran to her and sobbed my heart out, because I had missed her so much.

As I got older my father's violence towards me increased; he would hit me with a belt even for trivial offences, and I lived in constant fear of him. My older brother, however, was on the receiving end of the worst of the violence and I always witnessed it. Outwardly I was silent through fear, but inwardly there were times when outrage and hatred swelled to such a pitch that, had there been a weapon available, I might have done my dad a serious injury.

Inevitably, I suppose, my behaviour began to deteriorate. I started to do irrational things. For instance, on my way to school each day I passed a house where an elderly woman lived alone, and on several mornings I emptied her milk on to the doorstep; not in a vindictive or violent way, in fact I felt very calm about it. I got caught, of course, but that was one of the few things my dad didn't find out about.

At about this time, just before I went to secondary school, I had my first experience with a ouija-board at the youth club in the village hall, a typically shabby place used mostly for jumble sales. I didn't know what to expect, and didn't then understand that ouija-boards are to do with the occult and not to be meddled with. The experience was rather frightening but at the same time fascinating, and it was the start of an involvement with ouija-boards that was to last for years.

I hated secondary school—not as much as I hated being at home, but I hated it nevertheless. My behaviour got worse; in my first term I was caught smoking in the toilet during geography (I couldn't bear the teacher, who seemed to take a positive pleasure in humiliating me). I was given a detention but, to avoid a belting from my dad, told my parents I was captaining the hockey team after school. They were really pleased! My brother told them the truth, however, and I got several beltings—for smoking, lying, being put in detention, and a couple more for good measure. After such incidents I was too embarrassed about the marks on my body to shower with the other girls at school.

But the more I was punished the worse my behaviour became. When I was twelve I used my dinner money to buy sweets and cigarettes. I still went in for a school meal; I just didn't pay. The head found out and summoned me to his office, where my form mistress and the school supervisor had already gathered—like judge, jury and executioner rolled into one. They wanted to know if they or I should tell my parents.

When I said I would, the supervisor said he would call on them too.

I panicked; my only thought was to get away from Dad, so I sneaked out of school the back way, my heart beating in terror, and ran away. Fearing someone would recognise me, I climbed into an outhouse through a hole in the roof; it was cold and smelly. While I waited there for it to get dark, I tried to take my mind off everything (including the smell) by planning my future. Eventually, after what seemed like an eternity, it grew dark and I managed to climb out again—much more difficult than climbing in. Soon police cars pulled up behind me on the lonely country road, together with my dad's car; as the police were there, this was the one occasion that my father didn't punish me physically.

One Saturday morning at about this time I took my dad a cup of tea in bed; as I went in I realised he was hiding something under the mattress. Some time later, when my parents were out, I crept into the room to find out what he had hidden. It was a pile of pornographic magazines. I dropped the mattress and ran, but after that whenever I was alone in the house I looked at them. They had a horrible fascination for me, and I kept going back to them, finding them exciting and frightening at the same time. That was my introduction to what I, as a twelve-year-old, assumed always took place between a man and a woman. My opinion of my dad became even lower because of it, and it certainly lessened my feelings of my own worth.

Perhaps because of the problems at home I found it very difficult to make friends at school. My father had a reputation for being nasty, I was his daughter, so I was 'tarred with the same brush'—kids can be very cruel.

In addition I had become very withdrawn and kept away from other children; this seemed to make them even more antagonistic. They would taunt me about the contents of the sandwiches which I now took (we were too poor for me to have 'posh' packed lunches like theirs) until I could stand it no longer and just went without lunch, throwing my sandwiches into the hedge on the way home from school, until Dad found out...

One day when I had wandered off in the lunch-hour and was sitting on the playing-field by myself, someone came along and offered me my first 'smoke' of cannabis; I was thirteen. The cannabis made me feel light-headed and vacant, less aware of what was going on, so to me it seemed a good thing. I was soon drawn into a little group who smoked cannabis or 'dope', and sometimes afterwards we would play with a ouija-board or practise levitation.

For just one year I had a friend at school; her name was Jenny, and we could relate to each other as our home backgrounds were alike. She was a bad influence, however, introducing me to a set of people who were all involved with drugs, the occult and promiscuity. I lost my virginity at fourteen and, strangely, I cried, feeling that I really had lost something special. Jenny had to leave school as she became pregnant, so that was the end of my one friendship.

Soon after this I started sleep-walking; once Mum found me with a raincoat on inside out, and a pair of knickers on my head (I had obviously thought they were a hat), sitting on the window-ledge with the window wide open and my feet dangling over the edge. I suppose sleep-walking was a symptom of the insecurity and vulnerability I felt at the time, though I couldn't have expressed it in those words.

I was almost sixteen when I was allowed to go to a dance at the local air-base; I was amazed that my dad had agreed. Mum made me a long dress for it, but as I was leaving, Dad told me I had to be back by eleven o'clock. As the dance didn't start till nine, I knew it would barely have warmed up by Dad's deadline. So I stayed an hour longer than he had said, and managed to talk the band's drummer into taking me home in an interval. We got back just after midnight; the landing light was on and I saw my dad running downstairs. Panic! I had hoped to creep in undetected.

'Quick,' I said to the drummer, 'drive somewhere, anywhere, but quick!'

He drove up the lane at the back of our house, never dreaming that my dad would follow us in his car, his headlights shining in until I became hysterical, pleading with the bewildered drummer to lock his car doors. I watched in horror as my father dragged him out of the car and punched him repeatedly in the face and ribs. Next he dragged me out of the car by my hair, punching me and shouting abuse at me. I kept trying to tell him that nothing had happened, but each time he smacked me across the mouth with the back of his hand. This continued when we got home until my mum stopped him.

A week later he lay on the sofa dying.

I had come full circle; I was still sitting alone in the chapel porch and realised that I'd been talking to myself out loud. I felt empty, and somehow vacant. There was nothing else to do so I walked home again.

After that, I felt as if I were in a vacuum. I returned to school and took public exams within a few weeks, though I didn't make much effort with them. As soon as I had taken them, in the summer of 1972, I left home.

2

I went to Devizes to work in a hotel with living-in accommodation. For a year or so I worked in a succession of hotels all over the West Country, never staying in one place for very long: I invariably got the sack. This was mostly because while I was in Devizes I was introduced to the drug amphetamine sulphate, known as 'speed', which is a stimulant. I used to go to all-night parties, then straight on to work. Sometimes I went as long as three nights without sleep, but still worked during the day.

My performance as a waitress deteriorated somewhat and at times became exactly that—a performance. Once, working in a silver service restaurant, I was serving a customer his vegetables; I blinked, but my eyes wouldn't open immediately and the serving dish slipped off the palm of my hand on to the gentleman's plate. His trout with almonds worked its way off the plate into his lap and peas flew all over the table— every waitress's nightmare.

From Devizes I went to West Lavington and then to Cirencester, where I started taking LSD, an hallucinogenic drug. From there I went to Gloucester and then to Bristol. By this time I was seventeen.

The first thing I have any memory of at all in Bristol is a church. I was wandering around tired and hungry, outside Trinity Tabernacle in Lawrence Hill one night, although at the time I was not aware that the place was a church. Two people approached me and invited me into the building, offering me a cup of tea. I went with them, past an open door where there were a lot of people with their hands in the air, shouting and singing. I thought they were all 'nutters' and felt momentarily apprehensive, but my desire for a cup of tea and something to eat was greater than my fear.

The couple, Andrew and Kay, talked to me at length and were later joined by a younger man called Lawrence. On finding out that I had nowhere to go, the couple took me with them to their home somewhere in Bristol. They gave me a bedroom to myself. I don't know how long I was there. One night Andrew and Kay, who had by then told me they were Christians, went out, and while they were gone I overdosed deliberately. I couldn't have told you why I did it—maybe it was a way of seeking attention. I woke up in a small room in the Bristol Royal Infirmary wired up to some machine. Two men came and asked me lots of questions. I was eventually told that I was being sent to a psychiatric unit. I didn't care what happened to me. At seventeen, I'd just had enough and wanted to give up.

An ambulance took me to the General Hospital. They put me in a wheelchair and pushed me down long grey corridors that seemed to close in behind me. We came to a door opening on to a concrete bridge that led to the psychiatric wing; through double doors, then another set of double doors. A nurse pushed me into the ward and along to a cubicle. She drew the curtains round my bed, put me to bed, removed all my belongings and left me there. I slept. ...

Somebody was watching me. I could sense it. I didn't know how long I had slept, but I didn't want to wake up. I opened my eyes reluctantly and sure enough there was a woman sitting on a chair watching me.

'Hello, lovey,' she said, in a voice that for some reason made me want to cry, 'my name's Sue and I've been asked to sit with you for a bit.'

'Why?' I asked.

'Well, I'm a nurse and actually it's my first day here too.'

'Where are my clothes?'

'We had to take them away, lovey, just for a while.'

Somebody else came through the curtains with some pills and water.

'We just want you to take these and then we'll leave you to get up when you're ready,' he said.

I swallowed the pills and he and Sue left me by myself.

I stared at the curtains round the bed. They were green, as was the bed cover. I suddenly felt the need for a cigarette. Pushing back the bedclothes, I grabbed the stripy hospital dressing-gown and peered round the curtain. There was nobody else around, so I drew the curtains back and then had to sit down on the bed as I felt dizzy and light-headed. This wasn't like a normal hospital ward. There were another twelve beds all with tall wardrobe-type lockers at the side of each, and a stained carpet on the floor. I got up slowly and walked over to the windows. These had blocks to prevent them from being opened. A cigarette—I had to have a cigarette.

I walked towards the door. On the right was a cubicle that had been partitioned off. A very thin woman with greying hair was crawling on the floor. She wore a transparent plastic apron, and one hand clutched a green paper towel. She didn't even notice me watching her. I had to get that cigarette. I reached the corridor. Further along were the two sets of double doors I had been wheeled through when I arrived. I stood there, looking at the bridge. Between the two sets of doors was an observation window I hadn't noticed before. A man saw me and somebody came running from the room and took me by the arm.

'Where are you going?'

'I've got to have a cigarette,' I explained.

'Have you got any?'

'No!'

'Well, we'll have to see if we can find you some then, won't we? But you can't smoke in the ward. You'll have to come into the day-room.'

She led me further down the corridor to a room on the right, sat me in a chair and went to find me a cigarette.

The day-room was empty apart from the usual furniture—a television, tables, soft armchairs, some hard-back chairs and tall cylinder-type ashtrays. Half-finished puzzles lay on the tables, together with used cups and empty cigarette packets. The walls were stained yellow with nicotine and the whole place smelt stale.

The girl came back and handed me several cigarettes

and a box of matches. This nurse wasn't wearing uni-
form either. She sat down a few chairs away. I lit a
cigarette.

'Thanks,' I said.

There was a noise over by the door. It was that
woman again, crawling on the floor. With a sigh the girl
stood up, saying, 'Come on, Rosie, up we get. You
know you're not supposed to crawl on the floor,' and
took her away.

It was probably just as well that I didn't know then
that this was to be my home for the next seven months.
The whole place was depressing.

The unit comprised three floors. The middle floor
contained psychiatrists' offices and small wards with
four beds. These smaller wards were for patients who
were 'doing well' and didn't need to be watched. On the
top floor was a conference room, dining-room, occupational therapy room and other smaller rooms and
offices. At first I was completely overwhelmed, but
gradually became used to the layout. There were
twenty or so patients of different ages and I was probably the youngest. The saddest person there was Rosie
who seemed to be for ever crawling on the floor and
throwing her dinner around. She sometimes had quite a
wild look in her eyes, almost as if she were trying to
break out of herself but couldn't because she was
trapped in her body.

In those seven months I saw a lot of people come and
go. Some of them came back a second and even a third
time. My medication kept being changed. We had to
queue outside the office for our medication. Rosie
nearly always refused to swallow hers and Henry would
yell from his room for his medication and a cigarette.

23

He rarely emerged as he had bad abscesses on his legs. The staff used to confiscate his cigarettes because he kept burning holes in the bedclothes.

Everything took on a sort of greyness for me; my day-to-day existence seemed meaningless and empty. Each morning would start with medication, food and the inevitable cigarette, followed by an afternoon in the day-room smoking and drinking tea. If we didn't have visitors, the evening was spent wandering around the corridors and from room to room. I spent many evenings like that.

Andrew and Kay came to visit me a few times initially. I find it very difficult to remember what we talked about. Lawrence came twice and each time brought me a bunch of flowers. On his second visit he said he wouldn't be able to come any more as he was going away to a 'Bible school'. After that I had no visitors for months.

One thing that had a tremendous effect on me at this time was a book called *Joni*, which I came across in the day-room. It was the true story of a girl who had had a diving accident and become paralysed from the neck down as a result. In the book she talked about her struggle: not wanting to be alive, seeing no point in continuing. She eventually got to know Jesus through a friend and found the strength she needed to carry on. It was, up to that point, the most moving thing I had ever read. I cried as I read the book, though I felt a bit cynical about the Jesus bit. When I had finished reading Joni's story I didn't consciously think about it any more, but it came to my mind much later on, as I faced another crisis.

During the time I spent at the unit, I had several

sessions with a series of psychiatrists in one of the offices. That room in particular seemed very grey. One psychiatrist was a big man and although he was quietly spoken I found him very intimidating. He would sit behind his desk looking intently at me while I sat on the opposite side of the desk staring through the window, or at the light, or at the floor—anywhere but at him. He used to ask me so many questions but I gave him very few answers, mostly because I either didn't know how to, or couldn't face the answers anyway. One day I got tired of all the questions and felt cornered. I stood on my chair and jumped on to his desk giggling hysterically. I think I was trying to stop his probing into my mind, to shock him. He changed my medication yet again.

I liked Sue, the first nurse. She seemed to me really human, not detached like the rest. It wasn't just a job to her. Consequently, quite a few of the patients latched on to her. Sometimes she would come across me hiding in a corridor on the middle floor when I should have been in occupational therapy. It was a good place to sit, since hardly anyone went along that particular corridor.

The first time she found me there she said, 'Hello lovey. I've got to have a ciggy. Let's share one, shall we? You won't tell anyone, will you?'

As we sat sharing a cigarette she asked me if I would like to go and stay with her and her family for a weekend.

'I don't think they'll let me,' I replied.

'They will if you're with me, I expect. I'll ask them and see what they say.'

At the time I thought nothing of it, since I didn't really expect to be able to go.

One day the psychiatrist announced, 'We've decided it would be best to try you with ECT.'

I was already aware that they used this on some patients on a certain day each week. I had seen the cylinders and other equipment at the bottom of the beds, and on that day nobody was allowed back into the ward after breakfast until the afternoon.

ECT is electroconvulsive therapy. They give the patient an anaesthetic, then place electrodes on his temples and put a sort of wedge into the mouth. An electric current is passed through the body, which then convulses. All I can remember about the course of ECT treatment is lying on the bed afterwards with a tremendous headache and feeling in desperate need of a cigarette. It has been established that ECT can damage the memory, and I believe that the large areas in my life of which I have little or no memory are a result of that course of ECT.

I had been admitted to the unit after taking an overdose, yet despite medication and psychiatric treatment, I felt no better; life still seemed grey, empty and meaningless. So, after starting on the ECT, I began to keep in the corner of my mouth all the pills that they gave me at medication times, and only pretended to swallow them. I don't know how many there were, but one day I swallowed them all at the same time and went to hide in the attic room where spare cleaning stuff was kept. It was locked, so I just sat at the top of the cold stone stairs hoping that nobody would find me, and wondering if I'd used enough pills to take away the greyness once and for all.

Eventually I was found and rushed to the Royal Infirmary for a stomach pump. They kept me there for several days, then sent me back to the unit where they put me, heavily sedated, in an observation room next to the office. They let me have my cigarettes in the room and locked me in at night. Every now and then they gave me injections, which made me very sleepy. There was a window through which I was watched. I don't know how long I stayed in there, but they eventually let me out and gave me back my clothes. The ECT continued and so did my medication.

One day Sue came looking for me.

'You can come home with me,' she said, beaming all over her face—'next weekend. But only for one night at first.'

I couldn't believe it. I was actually going to get out of there for a night. Occasionally we went for accompanied walks as part of occupational therapy but the only other time I went out was on Monday mornings to cash the orders in the allowance book I had from Social Security, and then those of us who went were accompanied by the staff.

When the day came for me to go home with Sue, I was actually really scared. I didn't know her family and thought I would just feel awkward and in the way. I couldn't have been more wrong. David, Sue's husband, accepted me as though I had always been there and Sue was just so good and kind. She seemed like an angel in my life at that time. Whenever she appeared things seemed a bit brighter. They had three children, all of whom made me very welcome. They didn't resent me as I had expected them to. I slept on the floor in the little girl's bedroom, and Sue looked after all my pills and gave them to me at the appropriate times.

On returning to the hospital I started to be more aware of the other patients around me, and the staff too. I became friendly with a girl called Cathy who was a white South African. She was an epileptic and had tried to kill herself by slashing her wrists with a carpet knife. Her moods were very erratic. One moment she seemed to be cheerful and laughing, then she would become extremely depressed and aggressive. She was in her early twenties, and never had a visit from anyone all the time she was there, which was probably about three months.

Nancy was another patient, also in her early twenties. I think she had had some bad experiences with LSD. She used to sit cross-legged in the middle of a corridor, making up strange songs. Her eyes looked vacant, and she always wore a sort of sad half-smile on her face.

One girl, whose name I can't remember, had long flowing hair down to her waist. She always kept the curtains drawn round her bed and never seemed to stop crying and screaming out. There was no doubt that she was in her own personal hell. She had a new baby who was in the unit with her. When she wasn't behind the curtains I used to sit watching her. I thought she was beautiful. Some years later I was to encounter her just once more in very different circumstances.

Sadly, Rosie never seemed to get any better. I used to feel so sorry for her husband who visited her every day, sometimes twice. She never spoke. Sometimes she sat crying, and each day she seemed to get thinner.

Henry didn't change either. Whoever happened to be passing his open door would get an earful.

'Nurse, nurse—is that you, nurse? Where are my cigarettes? My legs hurt. Please get me a cigarette. Nurse! *Nurse!*'

I called the occupational therapist 'Valiant Vanessa'. She tried so hard to find new and interesting things for the patients to do, and never complained when people like me disappeared in the middle of a session.

When I had been in the unit for about four months I received a letter from my mum to say she was coming to see me. I got quite excited as the day for her visit approached, because I hadn't seen her for over a year.

On the day, I washed my hair, borrowed a skirt and top from Cathy and then waited for Mum. I was sitting by the big double doors so that I could see her when she came. She arrived at last. My younger brother and sister came in first, and then Mum. She kissed me on the cheek just as a man I didn't know came through the door.

'This is Paul,' Mum said, turning towards him, 'my new husband.'

Then, turning back to me, she remarked, 'Oh dear! You have let yourself go, haven't you?'

I was vaguely disappointed. I also felt threatened and inhibited in the presence of this other person whom I had never seen before. I took them upstairs to the conference room and left them while I went to make some tea. After closing the door I turned and stood for a moment looking out of the corridor window. The unit had a bit of lawn enclosed by a very high wire fence. There was a tennis court, obviously unused for years, with weeds growing through the cracks in the tarmac. A stone water fountain, which no longer worked, some wooden seats and a few trees completed the scene.

As I looked down a little girl came running towards one of the seats followed by her mum and dad, together with one of the patients. They all sat on the seat and I watched as the little girl climbed on to her mother's lap and the mother put her arms round her. There was a lump in my throat. Then I remembered I was supposed to be getting the tea, so I ran down the corridor to the dining-room.

As I returned to the conference room carrying the tray of tea I felt very distant from the family sitting there. I was a bit of an oddity; I didn't seem to fit in anywhere.

'Where did you two meet then?' I asked.

They looked at each other, then Mum smiled kindly and said, 'We met through an escort agency in Swindon.'

'Oh.' I didn't know what else to say really. It turned out that he had a council house in Devizes and she had moved there with my brother and sister after the wedding.

They stayed a little while, then they said they had to leave because they were going to a pantomime at the Hippodrome. It was nearly Christmas. I walked with them downstairs. Mum kissed me on the cheek.

'Bye then. Keep in touch, won't you?'

'Yes,' I said. 'Bye.'

After they had gone I went back upstairs to the conference room and sat down, lighting a cigarette. Panic began to rise inside me: I felt rejected again and, remembering the little girl whom I had seen from the window, held close on her mother's lap, I realised I wanted so much to be hugged and loved. I just continued smoking until somebody came to find me. They changed my medication again.

A short time later Cathy had a letter from her grandparents, who lived on a caravan site near Bridgwater.

'They've invited me to stay over Christmas; do you want to come? I know it's a while till Christmas, but they should let you out by then.'

'What if they don't?' I asked.

'Well, you can always discharge yourself, you know. That's what I'm going to do.'

I don't know why the thought had never occurred to me before. I hadn't realised that I could discharge myself. Oh, I knew I couldn't have done so for the first few months, but I'd been there for nearly six. For the next few days the thought was never far away. I had decided to discharge myself; it was just a matter of timing.

A little while before Christmas some entertainment was planned for the patients. Two men came and played a violin and a guitar and sang. I thought they sounded awful! We all had coffee afterwards, during which time Cathy got to know one of them. Each night for the following week or so he came to visit her. One night she came to find me.

'I'm off,' she announced. 'Are you coming?'

'Where are you going? Where will you stay?'

'Joe lives in a commune on the other side of Bristol. You can come if you want.'

Did I really want to? Yes, but I was afraid.

'OK,' I said, 'I'll tell them I want to discharge myself.'

When they knew I had somewhere to live they let me go, just like that, though a doctor saw me first and tried to talk me out of it. He eventually wrote up some medication for me to take. I signed a form, packed my few belongings and said goodbye to Rosie, who just looked at me wildly. I went to the office and was handed some little brown envelopes with different sorts of pills in. They said something about seeing a doctor, but I wasn't really listening. I was too scared.

I was standing by the double doors. Cathy and Joe were waiting outside. We walked together across the bridge, through the door and along the corridors to the front entrance. It was dark. We got into Joe's car and drove off. My heart was pounding madly.

3

I was sitting on the floor in a dimly-lit room with my back to the wall, rocking to and fro and clutching the brown envelopes containing my pills. There were several other people in the room talking, smoking dope and drinking. Music played loudly and there were occasional bursts of laughter.

I wished they would go away. I needed to think and couldn't. Anything could happen; this place didn't feel very safe. I began to regret discharging myself from the psychiatric unit, but knew I couldn't go back. Cathy had disappeared with another chap, saying she would keep in touch. Maybe if I took some pills I would feel less threatened. Nobody seemed to notice me stand up and walk across the room. I ran downstairs, locked myself in the bathroom and took some pills. Rolling a cigarette, I sat on the toilet and smoked. I still couldn't think straight, but it did seem that there was no choice for me but to stay. Where would I go if I left?

I went back upstairs. The noise had died down a bit and one or two people were sleeping. There was a space on a mattress in the corner, so I curled up there, thinking it would be almost impossible to fall asleep, but it wasn't and I soon drifted off.

During the next few weeks I learned a few things, such as how to make green lentil stew. I'm not really sure whether or not there was an art to making it or if it was an accident that it tasted different every time it was made. Sometimes it tasted like porridge; at other times it was delicious. Although it always tasted different, the colour was constant—always some shade of green. We did eat other things, but lentil stew was the cheapest meal to make.

I learnt other things too: how to obtain the maximum amount of money from Social Security for clothing grants, and about signing on under several different names. I learnt how to make home-brewed beer and lager, which everybody drank a few days after it was made, complete with sediment. It was foul.

At this point, I fell into a relationship with Joe. That's the only way to describe it. Looking back now I can see how empty and futile it was. It didn't take long for me to discover that he had been an alcoholic for several years. He would take Mandrax and Valium to enhance the effect of the alcohol. Everybody in the house used amphetamines and smoked dope, as did most of the people who came to visit. There were often 'parties' that went on for several days.

During one of these parties I decided to have a bath. The last thing I remember is lying back in the bath and lighting a cigarette. I must have blacked out. I came round in a very cold bath with tobacco and cigarette paper floating around, and was aware that somebody was trying to break down the bathroom door with an axe. I was so shocked that at first I just sat staring, but then I realised what must have happened and yelled at them to stop. We had all had a bit of a fright but not enough to prevent the parties from continuing.

A real mixture of people used to come to the house: students, hell's angels, a couple of nurses, several seemingly respectable married couples and a variety of hippies. I hadn't previously been aware that such a cross-section of people used and experimented with drugs.

Life went on like this for several months. Parties, people, drink, drugs and more parties. Then one morning I woke up with a terrific pain in my side. I didn't know what it was and didn't say anything about it all day, but just stayed out of the way. Eventually the pain became so bad that I was crying with it. I started to panic, and went downstairs, thinking perhaps I ought to tell someone. There were three people in the room, one of them a hell's angel, big and intimidating.

'I've got this pain in my side,' I gasped.

Tiny, the 'angel', looked at me as if I were some kind of pest that had wriggled its way out from under the floor boards.

Somebody said, 'You'd better sit down.'

'I can't,' I gasped.

Tiny got up, grabbed me by the shoulders and, gently for him, I suppose, shoved me on to the settee. I think I probably swore.

'Wot side does it 'urt?' he asked.

I showed him. He nodded knowingly, yanked my shirt up and poked a massive finger into the opposite side, then pulled it away again quickly. My body jerked and I yelled.

''Pendicitis,' pronounced Tiny, 'ambulance,' and

motioned for somebody to phone for an ambulance. He was a man of few words.

I refused to believe that it was my appendix and I wasn't going to get into an ambulance again for anything. I made my painful way back upstairs. Now what was I going to do? I was terrified of going into hospital. I peered round the door of somebody else's room to see if anybody was there. No one was so I hid in the wardrobe.

It was Tiny who found me. He picked me up and shouted, 'I got 'er.'

The ambulance men came upstairs with a wheelchair, carried me down and took me to hospital. It turned out that I had acute appendicitis, and they operated straight away.

The following day as I lay in a hospital bed recovering I saw Joe staggering into the ward carrying a giant suitcase. I couldn't decide whether he was staggering under the weight or whether he was drunk again. As it turned out I was right on both counts. He came to the side of the bed and stood grinning at me.

'I don't see what's so funny,' I said, 'and what have you got in there?'—pointing to the suitcase.

He put the suitcase across my legs. It was so heavy it made me wince. He opened the lid for me to see inside.

'What is it?'

'It's a synthesiser. I got a mixer as well, but I couldn't bring both.'

'But what did you bring this for, and where did you get it?'

He was grinning at me again. 'I got it from the organ centre up the road last night,' he said. 'I put an axe through the window.' He looked serious then. 'The thing is, I left the axe behind, so we'll have to shoot off somewhere else as soon as you're out of hospital.'

'How? We haven't got any money. Where will we go?'

'Don't you worry, I'll get some money,' and off he went, staggering back across the ward with his suitcase.

As soon as I was discharged we left Bristol and went to stay in a caravan just outside Torquay. We spent the next few months doing nothing much. Joe disappeared a couple of times, and each time came back with bags of stuff that he had stolen from houses he had broken into. His alcoholism and addiction to Valium were becoming progressively worse. I had to alter his prescriptions so that he could get more from the chemist. Eventually I was arrested in a chemist's shop and charged with forgery and obtaining drugs illegally. Up to that point I had had no criminal record.

We returned to Bristol. After a short stay in the commune we managed to find a small bed-sit with a tiny kitchen area. Its one saving grace was that it had french windows that opened on to a small yard.

Not long after we had moved into the bed-sit I discovered that I was pregnant. I was a very immature eighteen. I was shocked, and pretended to myself for a little while that it wasn't true, in the hope that I might be mistaken. I didn't know what to do. There seemed to me to be no alternative but to have an abortion, although I didn't know what it would entail. I hadn't talked to anyone about my situation. Once again, there didn't seem to be anyone I could talk to. I made an appointment to see a doctor, and decided I was going to tell him that I didn't want the baby, and that I wanted an abortion. When the day came for me to see him I felt quite strange, very robotic. My body and mind wanted to do this thing, but my heart seemed somehow to be objecting. I told the doctor what I had planned to say, without looking at him.

'Are you sure about this?' he asked.

'No, but I don't want the baby, and there's no other way.'

'Have you thought about adoption?'

I looked up. Of course. How stupid of me. I hadn't thought about adoption at all. The doctor talked to me further about what I felt, and I left the surgery with a lighter burden. The more I thought about it the more it seemed to make sense. I wouldn't have an abortion. Somebody else could have the baby, someone who really wanted a child.

I started seeing a social worker called Janet, who eventually became more like a friend. I missed several appointments for check-ups at the clinic, so on my first visit I was about five months pregnant. The midwife promptly told me off for not going before.

I went in to see the consultant. He felt my tummy, smiled at me and said, 'I think you're going to have twins, my dear. We'll send you for a scan.'

I couldn't believe it. This couldn't be happening to me. I left the clinic, went to the nearest pub and downed several pints of beer, then sat on a park bench and cried. I felt really frightened and alone. Janet, the social worker, was the only person who would understand. Joe didn't even seem to be aware of my existence most of the time.

One day Janet said I needed to see somebody who dealt with adoption and fostering. I remember little of the subsequent interview, but years later I discovered that the woman I saw was a Christian and that she had started to pray for me at that point when we had first met. God was doing something in my life, even though at that time I knew little about him and cared even less.

I had to go into hospital for the last two weeks of the pregnancy because I had very high blood pressure. The ward was full of women who seemed to talk about nothing but babies, baby clothes and their families, so I used to sit smoking in the day-room by myself. Joe came to see me a couple of times, but he was drunk. More than anything else I felt sad at visiting times. Most of the other women seemed so happy, and their happiness was shared with parents and husbands. I felt totally alone.

When I went into labour I was frightened. They took me down to the delivery suite. Joe was there, but they asked him to leave because he was drunk again.

As I was giving birth I felt an incredible mixture of joy, pain and sadness. The babies were both boys and they were beautiful. I expected the staff to take them away at once, but they didn't. As I looked at my babies I wondered how on earth I was going to leave the hospital without them. Then two nurses came and wheeled them away.

I was allowed a room to myself after the twins were born and had to stay in the hospital for two days. All the time I knew that the twins were in the nursery in the next ward.

I couldn't bear it. I had to see them. It was night-time. The nursery nurse showed me where they were, lying next to each other in little trolleys. I stood between the trolleys, put my little fingers into one of each of their hands, and stood like that for some time, with both babies clutching a little finger, and tears streaming down my face. I would call one Philip and the other Mark. The nursery nurse came and put a hand on my shoulder.

'Are you all right?' she asked gently. 'Would you like to feed one of them?'

I shook my head and rushed from the room. In the morning Janet came to pick me up, and I left Philip and Mark behind.

The next couple of days were dreadful. I had such an ache inside, and I couldn't concentrate on anything. All I could think of was the fact that I had left my children behind. I phoned Janet.

'I can't bear it, Janet. I've got to go and get them and at least try.'

'OK,' she said, 'I'll be there shortly.'

A few hours later she turned up. 'Are you sure about this?'

'Yes.'

She went out to the car and came back with a cot, a bag of baby clothes and bedding. On the way to the hospital we bought nappies, bottles and other necessities. I wouldn't have managed without her. We picked up Philip and Mark and I sat in the back of her car, cuddling them both for the first time.

Living in a small bed-sit with two babies and an alcoholic would be difficult, but I wanted and needed to try. We had registered for a council house, and had been waiting for several months. I had managed to get hold of another cot and all the other equipment that we needed and now all we could do was wait. For a little while Joe tried to sort out his drinking problem, but the improvement was short-lived.

We were eventually offered a three-bedroomed council house in Knowle West, Bristol. As we had no furniture of our own, we borrowed several mattresses and moved in with just the babies' things, our clothes, a cooker and various pots, pans and utensils.

After several weeks the Social Security department had supplied us with furniture, floor covering and curtain material. We even managed to get hold of a television set. Despite having the house, I hated living on the estate, partly because I was on my own so much. I didn't know anyone and it was quite a long way from the commune and the people there. Joe was out most of the time. When he wasn't actually drinking, he was busking to earn money for another drink.

Janet came to see me quite often, but apart from her there wasn't really anyone else. Jehovah's Witnesses knocked on the door one day and I felt so desperate for adult company that I let them in. They talked a lot and I listened, or rather gave the appearance of listening; I don't remember most of what was said. It just felt good to have someone else around. They told me that they visited everybody on the estate; some people invited them in but the majority didn't. Even though few people asked them in, they still persisted. I think I admired them for that. After the first visit they came a few times, and then the visits stopped. I felt quite let down, thinking it unlikely that anyone else would call. Joe continued to stay away from home. If he bothered coming back at all it was usually in the early hours of the morning.

One night I woke up, smelling burning. I turned on the light, and there was smoke in the room. I ran into the twins' room to make sure they were OK, opened their window, shut the door and went downstairs. The smoke was even worse down there. In the living-room Joe was lying face down on the floor. He was so drunk he had passed out. I opened the front door, dragged him outside and ran back into the living-room. Smoke was pouring from the kitchen—the cooker was on fire. I don't know how I managed it, but I put the fire out by myself, and opened all the windows to let the smoke out.

Then I sat down. It was five o'clock in the morning. I just sat there, smoking cigarettes and putting off thinking about it for a couple of hours. I'd left Joe outside and when I went to close the front door he had gone. It would soon be time to get the twins up. I went round shutting all the windows, thinking I ought to light a fire. It was only then that I noticed that my hands were filthy and my night-dress covered in soot.

Everything around me in the living-room was covered with a layer of soot, as was the hallway. It was the last straw. I couldn't face going into the kitchen to see what that was like. Sitting down on the floor, I lit another cigarette, and started to sob. I felt totally out of control and incapable of keeping everything together any longer. I finally plucked up courage to go into the kitchen, which was even worse than I'd expected. I found the twins' bottles; even they were filthy with soot. I washed them, boiled a kettle and made up their milk.

I realised that I had to do something about the situation: Philip and Mark were ten months old and had started crawling around all over the place. In tears, I took the bottles upstairs, changed the twins and gave them their milk. Then I pulled on some clothes, got the push-chair out and left the house with the twins, trying to think what to do.

I went to a call-box and phoned Janet, who arranged to meet me in a café. She was very good, not asking any questions until I'd finished my coffee, and could take her to the house. She suggested that I put Philip and Mark into temporary care in order to give me a chance to clean the house from top to bottom and decide what I was going to do. So they went to a foster home for a few days. Each day Janet picked me up to go and visit them.

Shortly after this, while he was drunk, Joe went to the police and told them about the burglaries he'd committed, and they kept him in custody. By this time my emotions were so deadened, except where the twins were concerned, that I hardly felt any reaction on hearing news of his detention.

I had a lot of time to think. Philip and Mark would soon be a year old, and they hadn't had much of a life in that first year, although I had tried hard. Maybe I should have had them adopted in the first place. I talked to Janet about it. She said she thought we should go and pick the twins up now that the house was reasonably clean again, and that I ought to see how I felt when they were home with me. That made sense to me, so that's what I did.

After a week I called Janet again.

'I've decided that the best thing I can do is have Philip and Mark adopted. Please help me.'

She did. Without her I would have gone under long before that. The children were made wards of court, although I was still able to visit them if I wanted to. So right up to the week before they were adopted, I continued to see them regularly. I just missed their first birthday, and they were officially adopted the day afterwards. The last time I saw them was on a beautiful sunny day. They were in a nursery with lots of other children. It somehow reminded me of that time in the hospital when I stood in the nursery holding their hands, except that this time they could see me. They looked at me with their lovely innocent eyes, smiled and came tottering uncertainly towards me with their little arms outstretched to be picked up. So I sat with one on one knee and one on the other, cuddling them and making them laugh. They didn't cry when I left and I felt strangely proud of them. I waved. They both waved back. I was determined not to cry, and I didn't for years afterwards, but I am crying as I write this now.

I went back to that house full of memories of Philip and Mark, sold most of the furniture and lived in the living-room. Over the next few weeks I applied for a number of jobs in the Cotswolds, to work in hotels, and went for several interviews. Eventually I had a letter offering me a job just outside Stroud in Gloucestershire. The following day I packed my suitcase. Before leaving the house I went upstairs to the twins' bedroom. One of the cots remained, still made up. Everything else of theirs had gone. I ran my hand along the side of the cot, then turned and left the room. I went downstairs, locked the front door and put the key through the letterbox, then walked up the path and down the road without looking back.

4

A song by Tracy Chapman starts with the words: 'All the bridges that you burn come back one day to haunt you.'

I suppose when I left Bristol that was what I was trying to do, in a sense—burn my bridges. I hoped that by moving away from where it had all happened I would be able to forget and put it behind me. What I failed to realise was that in this case the bridges were within me, so moving away didn't help; I still had to cope with my memories and mixed feelings about the twins.

There were very short periods of time when a combination of alcohol, dope and speed enabled me to suppress my thoughts and emotions. Then suddenly everything would come rushing back to the surface again. I couldn't hold down a job for any longer than a month at a time. I didn't know what to do with my thoughts and feelings. I couldn't talk to anyone; once again, when I needed somebody to talk to, there was no one.

A lot of my time was spent thinking about Philip and Mark, and it was always worse at night. They had often woken up in the night and I couldn't bear the thought that they might be crying for me. The only things I had brought from Bristol to remind me of them were photographs. I used to line them up on the bed and sit staring at them. Although I didn't seem able to cry or shout about it, there was what I can only describe as a great hollow, deep inside me, which seemed to cause almost physical pain. In the end I burnt all the photographs except two, which I sent to my mum with a brief letter of explanation. After that there was nothing left to remind me—except love, guilt, fear and a sense of failure.

I was afraid for Philip and Mark, afraid for their future. Question after question went through my mind. Had I done the right thing for them, or simply tried to make life easier for myself? Would they hate me as they grew up, believing that I had rejected them? Had I rejected them? Why had I kept them in the first place? Was it because they needed me or rather because I needed them?

At that time, and for a long time afterwards, I convinced myself that I had kept the twins because they needed me; now I believe it was because I needed them. I wanted to possess them, because I needed to be loved by someone who would love me unreservedly in return. Even after the adoption had gone through I desperately wanted to be sure of their love and acceptance in later years. I couldn't live with the thought of them rejecting me in their turn, and even hating me, so I wrote them a letter to be given to them on their eighteenth birthday. I can't remember what I wrote in that letter, but it did nothing to assuage the guilt that I felt. I was just as afraid after I had written it as I had been before.

There seemed no way to get rid of the fear and the guilt, but looking back now I'm not sure whether, had I been shown a way at that time, I would have wanted to be healed or made whole since, apart from memories, the guilt and fear were all that were left to me of Philip and Mark.

Even as I write now, fifteen years later, I am aware of still having a sense of responsibility for what may or may not happen to them, and of fear at the thought of having to face them if they should turn up one day.

A song by Paul Field has these words:

> Is anybody out there
> Who knows the way I feel?
> Is anybody out there
> Who can give a love that's real?

That sums up how I felt at the time; all those years ago there was nobody to offer hope, nobody to say 'I know someone who can help you'. Maybe it was my own fault for being so self-contained. During this period in my life, I never attempted to go into a church, although I did hover outside a few times.

In the end I reached a point where I realised that being away from Bristol wasn't making any difference at all to the way I felt. I had been trying in vain to anaesthetise myself through drinking, smoking dope, using speed, and moving around. After six months or so I headed back to Bristol once again, ready to be sucked into the events that followed.

5

I moved into temporary accommodation in a hostel just outside the St Paul's area of Bristol. After signing on at the Social Security office I spent the next few months drifting aimlessly, spending most of my time in pubs and illegal drinking clubs. It was at this time that I became involved with a man called John who lived in a flat in the middle of St Paul's with his sister-in-law, Sarah, and her daughter. It was Sarah's flat, and I moved in too.

A month or so after we first met, I learnt that both John and Sarah were 'junkies', that is, drug addicts who use drugs intravenously. They hadn't tried very hard to hide the fact. I remember watching them for the first time—Sarah sticking a syringe into a vein in her leg and John probing around in his foot. The veins in their hands and arms were no longer usable. This was largely due to the use of drugs such as Diconal, Palfium and morphine pills, which contain a lot of chalk. Even though the pills are crushed, mixed with water and filtered through cotton wool, there is still a large amount of chalk injected into the veins.

The first time I saw them having a fix I thought I was going to be sick.

'You can have some if you want,' said John, looking across at me. I shook my head. They became very different after having a fix, seemingly more relaxed, and unaware of what was going on around them. Several days later John asked me again if I wanted some.

'All right,' I said.

He didn't respond straight away, but concentrated on cleaning out his syringe. I watched as he mixed another fix in the spoon. First he put in a tiny amount of a cream-coloured powder—heroin. He then squeezed a drop of lemon juice and added the water, before lighting some matches and holding them under the spoon to 'cook' the liquid. I felt a tense, knotted sensation inside as I watched him draw the liquid through a tiny piece of cotton wool with the syringe.

'You're sure about this, are you?' he asked as he stood up and walked towards me.

I definitely had a lot of doubts, but nodded.

'So,' he said, 'you want to be a junkie, do you?' Without waiting for a reply he plunged the needle into the muscle at the top of my arm. I clenched my fists and said nothing. I felt a gradual sensation of being covered with something—almost smothered. I sat motionless for a little while and then was violently sick. That was how I spent the rest of the day and evening—vomiting

However, even though that first fix had made me ill, it wasn't long before I was using heroin and morphine regularly and injecting directly into a vein. At first, after the initial sickness, the drugs gave me a sense of well-being. It was a bit like being in a cocoon. I didn't have to think about anything. I was just 'pleasantly' drifting.

After a little while, however, the tiny amount that I was injecting each day stopped having the desired effect, and so the amounts were increased, until eventually, after nine months or so, it got to the point where I couldn't function without a fix. If I went longer than twelve hours I started to have withdrawal symptoms. As soon as I woke up I needed a fix. So it went on, with the number of fixes in a day increasing to three and then four.

John had been a junkie for a long time and had spent several years in penal institutions for drug-related crimes such as burglaries, chemist break-ins and assault. He had a very long criminal record and consequently was no longer prepared to take as many risks as he had once taken. I had only one previous conviction so I became the one who took most of the risks, partly because I was afraid of what John would do to me if I didn't.

Sometimes I thought John had a split personality. He could be very calm and charming, then suddenly for no apparent reason become very vicious. The first time I experienced being on the receiving end of violence from him was after we walked out of a pub one night. In the pub I had said hello to someone I vaguely knew. On leaving the pub John hit me so hard that I didn't feel the blow, but found myself lying on my back on the pavement. Several people stopped to look. I sat up.

'Did I walk into a lamppost or something?'

'No,' John said, 'you walked into my fist. Get up. You're making a fool of yourself.'

He walked on, and I stood up, following him slowly,

wondering what on earth I had done to make him so violent towards me. I should have run then, when I had the chance, but he would probably easily have caught me. He was waiting for me to catch him up. He looked normal enough, not angry or uptight and I told myself I would be all right.

As I reached him he grabbed my hair with both hands and dragged me further down the street. I screamed and lost my footing. Nobody was going to stop him. Eventually he stopped dragging me down the road, and I found myself sitting on the pavement, with my back to the wall and John squatting in front of me. He gently ran a finger down my cheek, then grabbed my hair again and started banging my head against the brick wall. Suddenly he stopped and, apparently realising what he was doing, pulled me to my feet, and we went home. I was too afraid not to go.

The following day my whole face was badly bruised and swollen and I made up my mind that once John had gone out I would leave. Sarah told me that she had received similar treatment. I felt sorry for her and didn't like leaving her by herself, so I gave her the address of the place where I was going, making her promise not to let John know. Sue, the nurse from the psychiatric unit, was the only person I knew of who could put me up. I left Sarah's flat, intending never to go back. Two days later John found me ...

There were other times when I didn't know what I had said or done to trigger John off. One afternoon we were all sitting in Sarah's living-room. There were ten or so barley-wine bottles on the table, some empty and some full. I made a casual remark and John suddenly picked up the bottles from the table and threw them at me, one by one, with great force. I was sitting in an armchair, so all I could do was shield my face. The bottles that hit me cut and scarred my legs. The ones that missed dented the wall and smashed.

I didn't know where I was with John from one minute to the next. The only time he was usually calm was after having a fix, although even then he was sometimes unpredictable. One such occasion was when a man called Dave came to see us. By this time we were dealing in drugs and lived in a flat on the top floor of a four-storey house in the St Paul's area. We effectively lived in just one room. There were several armchairs, a mattress on the floor, a television and very little else. John had taken to sleeping with a knife by the side of the bed, 'just in case'.

He had been probing around in his foot and leg for a good half-hour trying to find a vein, when the doorbell rang. I went through the usual procedure for identifying callers, and five minutes later Dave walked in. Most junkies I knew at this time were extremely thin and unhealthy-looking, but Dave was very well built and with his beard looked like a giant teddy bear. As he entered John finally managed to get a 'hit'.

'What can I do for you then, Dave?'

'Well,' responded Dave, grinning, 'I thought I might be able to do something for you.'

'Oh yeah! What could you do for me then?'

'I know where I can get some gear (heroin) and thought you might like me to get you some.'

'Where d'you get it from, Dave?'

'Oh, I can't tell you that.'

'No?'

At that point, the syringe still in his foot, John grabbed the knife and threw it just as Dave turned round. The knife struck him in the middle of his back. I couldn't believe my eyes. I just stood and watched the whole scene. John jumped up, pushed Dave through the door and down a flight of stairs. He then walked back into the flat, picked up the syringe, which had fallen out of his foot, and started again. I ran down the stairs and found Dave locked in his van. Luckily he had been wearing a thick leather jacket, so the knife hadn't done too much damage.

As time went on, because of many incidents like this one, I became really frightened of John. On two occasions he could easily have killed me. I was certainly too afraid to leave—anyway, I had nowhere else to go.

During the first two years in Bristol I think I must have received about twelve criminal convictions for theft, forgery and other drug-related offences. During that time too, many people I knew died, some through violence, some through overdoses and others because their bodies just couldn't take any more. Several times I witnessed a man completely stripped, trying to get a fix in his groin, and, failing this, probing open abscesses on his legs in the hope that he might hit a vein underneath.

Many people went into hospital for a quick cure. They usually went into psychiatric hospitals because there wasn't anywhere else. Others became psychiatric out-patients and were put on methadone programmes. Methadone is a drug given to addicts to wean them off heroin. Its big drawback is that it is more addictive than street heroin, since it doesn't contain any impurities.

By the end of those two years I started wanting to get

out of the situation. An opportunity presented itself when John was remanded in custody on charges of possession of drugs.

I went to the weekly drug out-patients' psychiatric clinic and told the psychiatrist the whole story. I was basically honest with him because I wanted help. His 'help' was to give me a prescription for a month's supply of the strongest type of methadone linctus. For a period of two weeks I stopped 'fixing' and used the bottle of methadone. The time after that my prescription only lasted four days. The temptation to use it all was too great. I have only ever known a few people stick with their prescribed amount.

After several months John was released on bail. In some ways I was quite relieved, but in other ways I wasn't. While John had been on remand I had had to find ways of smuggling drugs into the prison. So I was relieved that I no longer had to do that. When his case came up in court a few months later, he was sentenced to two years imprisonment suspended for two years. My own sentence for a related offence was two months imprisonment suspended for one year. We started dealing again only two or three days after appearing in court.

I still went to the clinic every week to pick up my prescription for methadone, and it was on one of these occasions that I bumped into the girl with the long flowing hair whom I had last seen, with her new baby, in the Susan Britton Wills psychiatric unit. As I came out of the clinic clutching my prescription in my coat pocket, she was standing just outside the entrance and I recognised her immediately, although I didn't know her name. She was wearing jeans and a stripy jumper.

When I walked out she looked straight at me and I remember feeling hesitant and vaguely uncomfortable. I told myself I was being paranoid, and that it was best just to pretend I hadn't seen her. I went to walk past her.

'Hello,' she said, moving towards me.

I smiled and before I could say anything she carried on.

'I used to have to go in there a lot you know, but they couldn't give me what I needed.'

'Oh,' I said, starting to move off slowly.

'It doesn't matter how many times or how often you go there, they won't be able to give you what you really need, you know.'

'That's all you know,' I thought, clenching the piece of paper in my pocket. 'What's she going on about?'

'I know somebody who can help you.'

'Do you?' I said. 'Well, I don't need any help.'

By this time I was walking so fast that it must have looked as if I were doing a funny walk, and she, to my mounting annoyance, was keeping up with me.

'I think you do. Jesus is the only person who can help you.'

I started a slow run then. She had stopped following me. Slowing to a quick walk again I glanced behind. She was standing looking at me.

'Jesus can change your whole life!' she shouted at my retreating back.

People had started to notice. 'What is this?' I thought.

'If you'll let him,' she yelled.

Next time I looked round, she was walking back to the hospital. I realise now that it was no coincidence that she was there that day just as I was leaving. God was speaking to me but I didn't want to know. I remembered the prescription in my pocket and my next fix.

Only a few weeks after this incident I realised that I was pregnant again. I didn't know whether to be happy or sad. I think there was probably still a part of me that wanted to have something of my own to possess and love, and maybe subconsciously that was why I had never thought about using the pill. I certainly hadn't considered what the consequences would be if I became pregnant while I was a drug addict.

At first I didn't tell anyone and as I considered the consequences for the child and myself (though admittedly more for myself) I was again in the position of having to decide what to do. Although I had managed to repress all thoughts and emotions connected with my past, I knew I would not be able to give birth to this baby and then have it adopted. I was thinking from a purely selfish point of view. Once again I considered having an abortion, but something seemed to hold me back from that.

I experienced the most peculiar feelings; I was afraid, and yet, because I was full of drugs, it was as if the fear became sectioned off into a little compartment in the back of my mind. Any thoughts about the physical effects of my addiction on the baby or what would happen to it after it was born were effectively relegated to this compartment, so when I considered adoption and abortion, it was in a very remote and detached way, almost as if I were half-heartedly considering someone else's situation.

I no longer had a social worker; I hadn't seen Janet since the twins were adopted. I did, however, have a probation officer called Aileen with whom I had a love-hate relationship: more hate than love initially. Aileen was a big Scottish woman who called a spade a spade. She took a lot of abuse from her clients, but gave as good as she got — and better!

I hadn't seen Aileen for several weeks. She drove past me in the street one day. The first indication I had of her presence was the squeal of brakes and the sound of a car reversing. She threw the passenger door open.

'Get in!' she shouted.

I started to walk in the opposite direction. Aileen got out of the car and yelled, 'If you don't get into this bloody car right now, then I'll have no hesitation whatsoever in having you up on two charges of breaching probation orders.' With that she clambered back into the car and slammed the door.

Needless to say I got in. She glared at me and offered me a cigarette. Aileen was like that, hard and soft at the same time.

'OK,' she said, starting the car, 'so why have you been avoiding me?'

'Have I?'

'You know damn well you have.'

'I'm pregnant.'

She didn't say anything, just stared straight ahead.

'Well, you did ask!' I said. 'You might at least say something.'

'We'll go back to the office and talk about it.'

So we did, although it was Aileen who did most of the talking. I came away from the office having agreed to see a different psychiatrist, who might be able to get me into hospital for a cure. I also had to see a midwife who turned out to be the one I had had for Philip and Mark. My relationship with her was definitely not good.

I did go into hospital for treatment for my drug addiction but even before I was admitted I knew I wouldn't stay. I was there for two weeks and John came to see me once a day with a fix. After two weeks, when the methadone had been drastically reduced, I discharged myself. The following few months went by very quickly, with me seeing Aileen and the midwife regularly—and remaining addicted to heroin.

I was seven-and-a-half months pregnant and had been in the most agonising pain for two days. After going out to get some drugs I managed to get indoors and crawl up three flights of stairs. 'If I can just have a fix, I'll be OK,' I thought. It took me a long time but in the end I managed it. John was worried and went to call an ambulance. I couldn't walk up and down; it was too painful, so I just lay down and waited.

John came with me to the maternity hospital. I had a severe kidney infection and had gone into premature labour. They had my notes, so they knew I was an addict. They set up a drip to stop the labour and gave me several injections of diamorphine for the pain. Calling John into the delivery suite they told him in front of me that I would have to stay in hospital for several weeks, that they would maintain me on methadone and that if he brought anything in the form of a fix into the hospital it could kill me. At the time I thought they were just trying to scare us, but John took it seriously.

I spent the first week in hospital under observation, receiving iron infusions, vitamin injections, sedatives and, of course, my methadone. At the end of two weeks I was discharged. I had kept to my methadone prescription and one fix a day, which just about kept me normal. Two weeks later I went into labour again and gave birth to a little girl.

In the few years since I had been an addict very little had broken through my selfishness and my need to block everything and everyone else out, but that little girl did. She was born addicted to heroin and spent the first eight weeks of her life in the special-care baby unit. She was sedated with Largactil and the doses were very slowly decreased. I stayed in the hospital for a week. When she was awake I fed and changed her. At first she could only take water; consequently she lost a lot of weight, but she gradually started to take milk. While she was asleep, I would sit beside her trolley watching her withdrawing from my drug addiction. Her tiny legs and arms would twitch and sometimes she would cry as she slept. I used to sit for hours just holding her in my arms. I don't remember ever crying. I only remember feeling remorseful that this innocent little girl should have to suffer because of me. I called her Joni, remembering the book that had made such an impression on me years before in the psychiatric unit.

Although Joni broke through my hardness, everything else I thought and felt, except the remorse, still went into that little compartment.

A week after giving birth to Joni, I was discharged, but went into the hospital twice a day to see her. Throughout this time I was still using drugs. In the first fortnight I seemed to spend a lot of time wandering into empty churches, sitting in a pew and gazing at nothing, feeling remorse twisting like a knot in my stomach—a very physical, almost tangible thing, yet I didn't know how to handle it or get rid of it. I couldn't cry or talk about it. It was as if I were dead inside, apart from this feeling.

One evening, on my way back from a visit to the hospital to see Joni, I was walking past a Salvation Army place and thought I heard singing. I stood on the step and looked through the glass pane in the door. Yes, they were singing. I thought I would just stand there for a little while and listen, when suddenly the door swung open and from inside a man said, 'You can come inside if you want to.'

I shook my head, still standing on the step.

'Are you sure?'

I nodded.

'OK.' The door swung shut again. I stayed on the step for a little while afterwards, feeling strangely sad. I didn't understand why I felt like that. After all, I hadn't wanted to go into the building and I hadn't wanted that man to talk to me. Or had I?

After sitting in a church one day I wrote to Mum, telling her about Joni, but not about any of the circumstances. I hadn't seen my mother or had any contact with her since the day she had visited me in the Susan Britton Wills unit. After writing and posting the letter I promptly forgot about it and was therefore surprised to receive a letter from her saying she was coming to see us the following Saturday. She arrived, and we went to the hospital to see Joni and then she went home again. She knew nothing about why Joni was still in hospital, or about my life.

From that point things just seemed to go from bad to worse. John became more violent towards me, although he never touched Joni in that way. I was horrified, therefore, when I came home one day to find John pacing up and down agitatedly.

'I've just phoned Smithson. They're going to come and take the kid away,' he said.

I couldn't believe my ears. Was this some kind of sick joke?

'You must be joking! You'd never do that.'

The doorbell rang and, sure enough, it was Alec Smithson, the social worker. He walked into the room followed by John, just as I picked Joni up from her cradle. Everyone sat down and only John seemed to know what was happening.

'Well, it's like this, see, Alec. I can't stand it any more and she'—pointing to me—'can't stand it either. She needs to go into hospital, and so do I.'

At that point John started to cry. He rolled up his trousers and showed Alec Smithson his puffed-up feet.

'Look at that, look at it. Soon there won't be any veins left.'

He grabbed one of my arms.

'Look at this mess. You've got to help us, Alec; you've got to take the kid away.'

Alec was looking at me. 'Is that what you want?'

I glanced at John warily and shook my head.

'Do you want a chance to get yourself sorted out?'

I nodded.

'Well, you could put Joni into voluntary care. You could go in for a proper cure and then you could have her back.'

'How can I be sure I'll get her back though?'

'All you have to do is give us twenty-four hours'

notice to say you're going to pick her up and take her home.'

John was watching me. 'It's the only way,' he said.

After a short silence I asked Mr Smithson how long it would take before they came to fetch Joni.

'We can do it straight away,' he said.

'OK.'

'I'll be back in two hours with the form and to give you the address of the foster-parents she'll be staying with.'

'OK.'

He left then and John went out shortly afterwards. I sat by the cradle holding Joni in my lap for nearly two hours, looking at her face and waiting for them to come back. Maybe part of me thought I might never get her back, but I wasn't conscious of thinking anything.

John got back first, only a few minutes before the social workers arrived. I signed the piece of paper, was told I could see Joni any time I liked as long as it was convenient for the foster-parents, and then the social workers left, taking a few of Joni's things with them. I went into the empty room at the front of the house and looked out of the window to the street below. They walked out of the front door with Joni and her teddy, and I watched them drive away.

The following day we both went to the clinic. The doctor said there weren't any places available in hospital and that we would have to wait. If we went back the following week they might be able to do something. He gave us both prescriptions for methadone until then. Before that point I hadn't even realised that it was nearly Christmas. Every other day in the week that followed I went by bus to see Joni. I hated walking into somebody else's house to see my little girl, but even more I hated coming away after an hour or two. I stuck to using just my prescription for that week, although John didn't. We went back to the clinic, only to be told that they could still do nothing except give us another prescription, but this time it would be reduced.

On leaving the hospital I bought a tiny Christmas tree, some cheap lights and one or two bits of tinsel. I took them home and put the Christmas tree up. When John came in I told him I was going to get Joni home for Christmas, half afraid that he would go mad, but he didn't. The next day I went out to find Joni a Christmas present, and bought her a big red caterpillar that moved along the floor. I took it home, wrapped it up and put it under the tree. It was the only present there, but that didn't matter. After that I went out to the call-box to ring Alec Smithson.

'I'm just calling to let you know that in twenty-four hours I'd like to pick Joni up.'

He was quiet for a moment and then said, 'OK.'

When I went to pick her up the following day, the social worker was at the house.

'I'm afraid you can't take her home at the moment. We're not satisfied that your home situation has changed. We have therefore obtained a court order giving us care and control.'

I left the house, got on a bus and went home. When I told John what had happened he went out, slamming the door behind him. I sat passively for a long time. After a while I opened the window, calmly picked up the Christmas tree, pushed it out and watched it fall four floors down. I went to get a fix.

The next day Mr Smithson called. When he walked

in John picked him up and threw him into Joni's cradle, breaking his glasses in the process. He didn't come back to the flat again.

After that I saw Joni very irregularly and we continued drug dealing, until in the end we owed money to the people who supplied us. John was also wanted by the police again. We took all the money and drugs we had and went to London, leaving everything else in the flat. After one weekend we thought we ought to go and see our suppliers, so we returned to the flat in Bristol. It had been broken into and everything smashed. There was a note on the door that read: 'We'll get the kid.' There was no way they could have got Joni since nobody knew where she was except the social services and us. It could have been an attempt to scare us. If it was, it worked. Joni, too, was shoved into that little compartment at the back of my mind and within a week John and I were on a boat to Amsterdam.

6

It was night when we arrived at the central station in Amsterdam. Though it was late the station appeared to be very busy. One of the first things I noticed was that there were several armed policemen around, which didn't exactly fill me with a sense of security!

We had the address of two contacts, Paul and Chris, on the run from the British police, so all we had to do was find the boarding-house where they were staying. As we crossed the road outside the station I noticed what looked like some kind of café, lit solely by candle-light. I felt quite drawn to it and would have liked to go and see what the place was like, but we had to find the house. I remember thinking that perhaps I would go there another time.

It didn't take us long to find the house, in a narrow street with shops and cafés on either side. On entering we found ourselves in an extremely dingy-looking bar. We were led down a dimly-lit, narrow passage and then up some stairs to the first floor. The whole place smelled of stale beer and urine. I don't know how many people shared what served as a bathroom, but I don't think it had been cleaned in a long time. The room we rented was tiny and contained a bed, a chair and a dressing-table. On the floor was a stained square of carpet, frayed at the edges.

We booked in indefinitely, although money was limited and the drugs we had brought with us were unlikely to last much longer than a week. The place seemed to be full of villains and junkies. There may have been some above-board people staying there, but if there were I certainly didn't notice them!

Paul and John started having arguments over the best ways to get some money. Paul was as difficult to communicate with as John. He was more violent and extremely paranoid. About half-way through the second week John and Paul had a violent argument in the street at the front of the boarding-house. Suddenly Paul dived at John, pushing him through a huge plate-glass window. A small crowd was gathering and Paul, who had landed on top of John, got up and ran off. John lay in the glass with a long and very deep gash in his side.

I heard a siren. Thinking it was the police, I ran down the alley at the side of the boarding-house, in through a side door and up the stairs to our room. I took our passports from under the mattress, a syringe and the heroin that was meant for our next fix. Before leaving I looked out of the window; it wasn't the police, but an ambulance, and John was being carried to it on a stretcher. I knew it wouldn't be long before the police arrived though, so I left everything else, ran down the stairs and out through the side entrance again. If they discovered John's identity they would deport him and the chances were they would deport me too.

'I shouldn't have panicked,' I thought. 'I should have brought some more clothes, a coat, or even some proper shoes.' As it was, all I was wearing was a flimsy summer dress and high-heeled sandals—hardly the right kind of gear for sleeping out, which was what I would have to do.

I needed somewhere to think, so I sat in a café and ordered coffee. What could I do? I had the equivalent of about five pounds in Dutch guilders, two passports and two fixes. I left the table and went to the toilet to have a fix, at the same time deciding that I would have to sell the passports. I knew a place where I could get rid of them but didn't relish the thought of going there. I wasn't thinking in the long term at all. All I was worried about was where my drug supply would come from in the next few days.

The money from the sale of the passports kept me in drugs, cigarettes and coffee for some days. At night, when I wasn't wandering around the streets, I slept on some boarding down by the canal almost opposite the station. I think it was some kind of old jetty. At first I didn't seem to feel the cold. As long as I had my fix I was all right. There were always other people, alcoholics mostly, trying to sleep there.

Sometimes I spent so long at night looking at the rippling blackness of the water that it seemed to draw me towards it. The smell of the place was not very pleasant, but I don't suppose I smelt very pleasant myself.

John had been discharged from hospital with numerous stitches in his side. It didn't take him long to find me. He decided that we would both stand a better chance of avoiding the police if we separated. I was very relieved.

The money had gone. Even my shoes had gone—I'd

had to take them off to run away from someone. All I had left were the clothes I had been wearing since leaving the boarding-house. I hadn't washed in that time, except my face and hands.

It was night-time and I was walking again, barefoot. At that time walking and sitting on the jetty were all I ever seemed to do, but at least before I hadn't noticed so much. I noticed now because I hadn't had a fix all day. I was thirsty and my feet hurt.

I walked over to some tourists who were sitting at a table outside a café, smoking and drinking.

'Can you spare a cigarette?'

They gave me several, which was encouraging.

'Could you spare a guilder for a cup of coffee?'

I was surprised when they gave me a guilder. That was when I started begging.

'Please, can you spare a guilder for a cup of coffee?'

I knew I'd never get enough money for a fix this way and I couldn't take anybody's bag or wallet because I felt too ill to run fast enough. At least I would be able to buy some tobacco and some coffee, so I went on: 'Please, can you spare a guilder for a cup of coffee?'

I didn't need to try to look pathetic! I remember approaching a middle-aged man in a suit. He spoke with a Birmingham accent.

'Oh come on, luv. Pull the other one, it can't be that bad.'

It was.

I shrugged and wandered off. It started to rain. Before long I'd collected enough for my tobacco. I went and sat on the jetty, rolled a cigarette and lit it. It was cold and yet I was sweating. I moved closer to the wall. Thoughts were rushing through my mind: *Why did I come here? Will I die in this place? Would anybody even notice if I did?* I shivered. If only there were somewhere warmer to sit. Then I remembered the building I had seen on the night of our arrival—the place with a ground floor lit by candles. It was only a short distance away, and it might be a café. I might have enough for a cup of coffee.

I stood outside looking in through the window. There were tables and chairs and one candle on each table. It was empty, but the door was open and I went in. Even though it was much warmer inside I was still shivering as I sat down at one of the tables. A girl was coming towards me.

'Hello. Would you like a coffee?'

'I don't know. How much is it?'

'The first one is free. Would you like one?'

I was a bit surprised. No café I had ever been into gave coffee away for nothing.

'Yes,' I said. 'Yes please.'

She smiled and went to get it. I had started getting cramp in my stomach and was still shaking, but I felt strangely peaceful sitting in that place. The girl came back with my coffee.

'Thanks,' I said, as she put the coffee on the table in front of me.

'Do you want to be by yourself, or would you like someone to chat to?'

'I don't want to talk to anybody.'

'Shall I just sit with you then?'

I looked at her face. Her eyes were happy and she was smiling. I had an impression that she cared and I was aware of warmth from her. I nodded.

'OK,' I said.

I didn't know the girl's name, but she sat with me at

71

the table, neither of us speaking, while I drank my coffee. It wasn't an uncomfortable silence. It was good to sit with someone, to have, even for a short time, a companion who expected nothing from me. In fact, I almost felt that she was giving something to me.

The café itself wasn't spectacular. It seemed to have the bare minimum of furnishings, just tables, chairs, plants, flowers and on the walls several pictures with words in English underneath. One picture caught my attention. It was of a stream with green fields, flowers and a girl sitting by the stream; a picture of tranquillity.

I was distracted by the cramp in my stomach and had started going hot and cold again.

'Would you like another cup of coffee?' the girl asked.

'I'm not sure if I've got enough...'

'Don't worry. It doesn't matter at all. I'll go and get you a cup.'

While she was gone I looked at the picture again. This time I read the words as well:

> The Lord is my shepherd. I shall not be in want. He makes me lie down in green pastures; he leads me beside quiet waters; he restores my soul.

I didn't know what the words meant but there was something about them...

The girl came back with my coffee; I drank it quickly and stood up.

'I've got to go now. Thanks for the coffee.'

I walked to the door. She was still sitting at the table watching me.

'Thanks for sitting with me,' I said and, not giving her a chance to answer, I left.

I was on my way back to the place where I had been spending the nights when I bumped into someone I had met at the boarding-house, a friend of Paul and Chris's from Liverpool.

'You look a mess,' he said. 'Where have you been?'

'Nowhere.'

'Come on—I've had a good few days. I'll give you a fix.'

So I went with Scooby, who gave me a fix and something to eat before we parted company and I went back to my space on the jetty by the canal. At least the stomach cramp had gone and wouldn't return until the morning.

As I sat, leaning against the wall and staring at the water, I thought about the café I'd been into and wondered vaguely why it was there. Looking at the blackness of the water reminded me of the picture I had seen. I remember thinking how ironic those words seemed: '...I shall not be in want. He makes me lie down in green pastures; he leads me beside still waters...'

I was ill again almost as soon as I woke up and spent the whole day on my 'bed'. By evening I was starting to panic. I had to get either a fix or some help. I wasn't capable of doing the former and felt a need to talk to the girl who had sat with me the previous evening. I made my way to the café. This time there were a few people around. I sat down at a table, but I couldn't see the girl anywhere. A young man approached me.

'Are you looking for somebody?'

'There was a girl here last night. I thought she might be here again tonight.'

'You look as if you could do with a coffee,' he said. 'I'll get you one and then I'll try to find out who was working last night.'

He was a friendly man with a shock of red hair and huge eyes, which I instinctively avoided when he talked to me. He came back with my coffee.

'I'm sorry. I can't seem to find out who it was you saw.'

He sat down.

'You look as if you've been having a bit of a rough time. Do you want to talk to me about it?'

I don't know what it was about him that made me talk, but I did. I didn't tell him much, only about the previous few weeks. After I'd finished he asked me my name and I told him.

'My name's Ben,' he said. 'I'm married and we have a baby girl. Look, this might sound strange to you, but how would you feel about coming to stay with us for a few nights?'

I must have looked quite startled because he said, 'You don't have to answer me now. Why don't you sit here for a while and think about it and I'll go and discuss it with my wife.'

I nodded.

'Good. If you want any coffee or anything, just ask. I won't be long,' and off he went.

I sat thinking how lovely it would be to sleep in a bed, but I couldn't understand why this chap and his wife would want to help a complete stranger and a junkie at that. Ben came back with his wife, Emily, and their daughter. We were introduced and Emily told me how much she would like me to go and stay with them.

They took me back to their flat, which was at the top of a tall narrow building. It was tiny, consisting of a reasonably-sized living area with a small kitchenette, a tiny shower room and their bedroom in the roof. A small ladder went up to a square hole that led to the bedroom. I don't know what I was expecting, but I was surprised by the size of the flat and touched that they should want to share it with me. There was a spare bed in a corner, which was my space. The first thing Emily did was to give me a night-dress, a change of clothes, and a towel, flannel and soap, before sending me into the shower. I was so grateful to be able to take off the clothes I had been wearing for such a long time. I showered, washed my hair and changed. I put the night-dress on and when I came out of the shower room Emily handed me a pair of moccasins.

Everything was happening so fast that I hadn't had time to think or ask questions. I lay down on the bed while Ben and Emily sat at the small wooden breakfast table, drinking coffee.

'Who are you?' I asked. 'And why do you want to help me?'

Ben explained that they were both Christians from England and that they had been in Amsterdam for a year. They believed that God wanted them to work with people like me. The whole house was lived in by missionaries from different countries, all working at different places in the city.

Over the next couple of days I became very ill. Ben and Emily, with the help of two other people in the house, carried me downstairs and drove me to a hospital, which refused to admit me on the grounds that I didn't have any insurance. If I had had an accident, they would have been able to admit me. Ben argued with them but all they would do was give him four pills for me to take. They drove me back to the flat.

The few days that followed are a rather hazy memory, but I remember Ben praying over me as I was lying in bed. There were two other people in the room who also appeared to be praying. I felt I had lost control of the situation and I was frightened. I noticed for the first time that there were several black china dogs in the room. Ben noticed me looking at them and told someone to put them away. He then took out his Bible and said, 'I think she's possessed by a spirit of Jezebel.'

I was really frightened then. I screamed. The door opened and somebody came in. Somebody else said, 'Did you hear the scream?'

The next thing I knew everybody except Emily had gone. Nobody said anything about what was happening. Emily was holding my hand and she told me that they had been praying for my deliverance. I didn't understand. Ben then came into the room and looked at me.

'Yes,' he said, 'you look different. It's your eyes.'

I didn't know what to think. I didn't feel any different, and as far as I could tell nothing had changed.

I'm sure that they had my best interests at heart and believed that what they were doing was right, but looking back now I don't believe they really knew what they were doing.

Some time after this I was sitting in bed holding the baby, when Ben came back with a green piece of paper in his hand. The previous evening he had asked me about my passport. I had told him that it had been stolen from the boarding-house we had been staying in. He put the green paper on the bed and took the baby from me.

'I went to the police and reported your passport stolen. I made a statement on your behalf, explaining that you were ill.'

I looked at the piece of paper with the official stamp of the Dutch police on it.

'All you have to do is show that instead of your passport.'

'But I don't have the money to go back to England, and anyway, if I go back I'll have to go to court.'

'I know; we'll give you the money. In fact, we'll come back with you and take a week's holiday. I do think you should go back.'

I hadn't had a fix for about ten days. I knew if I went back to Bristol that that situation couldn't last, just as it wouldn't if I left Ben and Emily's flat and walked back into the streets of Amsterdam. I don't know why I didn't tell them that; perhaps I'd got too accustomed to not talking to anyone.

'When do you want to go?' I asked.

'In two days. Don't worry, we'll drop you off somewhere.'

7

Two days later we boarded a ferry to Dover. I was still ill and rather weak from being in bed. The journey back was a nightmare. I couldn't seem to stop vomiting. Compared to the journey out it seemed to take an incredibly long time. Eventually we docked in Dover. Ben and Emily drove me from Dover to Bristol. When we got there Ben asked me where I wanted them to drop me.

'St Paul's,' I said.

He looked at me, frowning. 'Are you sure?'

'Yes.'

They drove me to St Paul's. Emily kissed me good-bye with tears in her eyes. Ben gave me a hug, told me to take care, got back into the car and drove off. I stood on the pavement for a little while after they had gone; then I went to get a fix.

Shortly after arriving back in Bristol, I had to go to court; I was bailed but a condition of the bail was that I should stay in a probation hostel. Then I realised I was about four months pregnant. I was appalled and just wanted to die. I only ever left the hostel to get drugs and when I got back I would just shut myself in my room. The place was a mess, but I simply didn't care any more. I didn't think of the baby at all. I didn't turn up for appointments to see Aileen, my probation officer, who had contacted the midwife I had had previously and told her I was pregnant.

One day, when I was about six months pregnant, the midwife arrived on the doorstep. She just kept ringing the bell until I crawled out of bed to the window to see who it was.

'Go away!' I yelled.

'If you don't let me in,' came the reply, 'I'm going straight to the police and I'll arrange for you to be "sectioned" into a psychiatric hospital.'

That did it. I had no doubt at all that she would carry out her threat. I threw down the keys, crawled back into bed and waited for her to let herself in. She was Irish, short with dark hair, and wore a very hard expression. She came in, sat on the bed and looked at me.

'You need to get into hospital. I'll phone the maternity hospital and get you in there. They'll probably put you in isolation to begin with.' Suddenly she took my hand, and her expression softened as she said, 'You'll be OK.'

By the middle of that afternoon I was in hospital again. They put me in a room by myself and tested me for hepatitis amongst other things. I ate from paper plates, drank from plastic cups and everything was thrown away when I'd finished with it. I even had my own toilet that nobody else was allowed to use. Initially I had to be maintained on injections because I kept vomiting. After a week or so I was able to keep down the methadone linctus. Several people came to see me, including the solicitor who was working on Joni's case (she was still a ward of court); Aileen came a few times, and there was a new social worker. I must have seen somebody dealing with adoption. I still hadn't really thought about the baby I was carrying. I had decided to have it adopted immediately and made up my mind not to see it at all after it was born.

I gave birth to another little girl. A nurse wheeled her straight away to the special-care baby unit. I went back to the antenatal ward and stayed in my room most of the time. Two days later I walked down to the baby unit and asked where my little girl was. They showed me. She had black hair and was a very long baby. She, like Joni, was suffering withdrawals but it didn't seem to penetrate me somehow. I just felt dead inside. In the week that followed I went to look at her every day, but it wasn't until the last day that I picked her up. I wanted to give her a really pretty name before I left. I hugged her tightly to me while I thought. I called her Calandra.

At the time I didn't recognise any emotions about Calandra. I don't believe I allowed myself to feel any. Looking back now I think I was afraid. I knew I wouldn't be able to look after her and I also knew that the authorities could make it very difficult for me anyway, especially with Joni in care. More than anything else I was afraid even to hold her, apart from that one time, because I knew that if I did I would have to feel something.

During the months that followed I stayed in several places, the worst being an empty shell of a building, parts of which were blackened from fire. A number of other junkies lived there as well.

I was on a two-year suspended prison sentence with four charges pending. The last time I had appeared in court one of the conditions of bail was that I didn't enter two areas in the city; consequently my supplies were gradually being cut off. It was at this time that I met again a man called Barry, in the basement of a supplier's house. Though I didn't know it, that meeting was ultimately to change my life. God hadn't given up on me, though I had almost given up on myself.

'I haven't seen you around for a long time,' I said. 'Where have you been?'

'Oh, you know how it is with me. I use for a bit, then stop for a bit, only I don't seem to be able to do that any more.'

'I've never been able to do it,' I said. 'To be honest, I don't know how much longer I can last. Something's got to give; I can't handle it any more.'

Barry looked at me intently. 'Do you mean that?'

'Of course I mean it. I wouldn't say it otherwise.' I laughed. 'Maybe I would though.'

'Look,' he said, 'here's the telephone number of a guy I know who could help you. But you'd really have to mean it. He's in probation.'

'Thanks,' I said.

I kept the slip of paper for several days and then decided to phone the number.

Harry Coad came on the line.

'Hello. A guy called Barry Harris has given me your number. He said you might help me. I want to get off junk.'

'OK. I can see you. But I can't promise you anything. You'll have to come to my office.'

We made an appointment. When the day came I

phoned him up from a flat where I had been staying for a few days. 'Look, I can't make our appointment. I don't have the bus fare. Can we make it another day?'

'Carole, if you're really serious you'll get here at the time we said. If you can scrape together the money for a fix then you can certainly find the money or method to get here, so I shall still expect to see you.'

I put the phone down. Liz, the woman I was staying with, drove me to Harry's office in her car and even came in with me to see him. He was a big man, slightly balding, wearing glasses and a cream suit. He spoke in a very authoritative manner with a trace of a West Country accent. Liz and I sat down. Harry started to tell me about an organisation called the Coke Hole Trust. I don't remember much of the conversation, but I didn't feel threatened by him. Although he spoke authoritatively, he was also gentle. He told me that the Coke Hole Trust had a house that was run by Christians and was used specifically for the rehabilitation of female drug addicts.

'If you really want to go there,' Harry explained, 'you'll have to write them a very convincing letter. There is only one in the country, and I don't know if they have any places. Everything has to come from you.'

He gave me the address to write to. I kept the address but didn't do anything about it until I had a row with Liz and walked out. I hadn't seen my nurse-friend Sue for some years, but I knew that she would put me up. While I was there I wrote my letter. In the meantime, I knew a doctor who was keeping me in as many pills as I needed to keep withdrawals at bay. I had several conversations with Harry, who told me that there were places available.

After about a week I received a phone call from Coke Hole asking me to go down to Andover for an interview. I immediately contacted Aileen, who arranged for probation to pay the train fare. I felt dreadfully nervous and anxious on the journey down. I was picked up at the station by the senior social worker, who didn't look or act at all like my idea of a social worker. Sue and a guy called Mike, who worked in the house, interviewed me. The only question I can remember Sue asking me during the whole interview was, 'What moves you?'

I stared out of the window, desperately trying to find an answer to that question.

'What moves me? I don't know,' I thought. 'I can't think of anything.'

I knew that my answers to her questions would determine whether or not they would accept me, so I really wanted to answer the question. But I couldn't. I really didn't know what moved me.

I felt as if I'd messed up the whole interview, and during the following three days convinced myself that I wouldn't get a place. I had to phone up to tell them if I was still interested after the three days were up, and they would then tell me if they wanted me there. I dialled the number of Ashley Copse (the name of the house) and spoke to Judy, who was one of the house-parents.

'I'm still interested,' I said.

'Well, we feel we'd like you to come, but you need to get yourself in for detoxification. How long do you think that would take?'

'I don't know. There's usually a long waiting-list. I'll have to find out.'

'All right,' she said, 'keep in touch with us and let us know when you go in.'

I felt more positive than I had done for ages. The problem was going to be getting into a hospital first. Coke Hole only took people who were drug-free.

I went to the doctor and was absolutely amazed when he told me I could go in for detoxification the following day, but dismayed when he told me *where* I was going.

'The only place we can get you into is the Susan Britton Wills unit.' My heart sank! I couldn't believe it. Why couldn't it have been somewhere else—anywhere but there? I was very nervous by this time, partly because of where I was having to go, but mostly because in two weeks time I had another court appearance and I knew that I could be sent to prison. Sue Grandfield, the social worker attached to Coke Hole, was writing a letter to the court, but I didn't really know what my chances were. The next day I arrived at the hospital unit with my few belongings, feeling once again that I had little control over what would happen next in my life.

Nothing had changed except that Rosie and Henry were no longer there, and there had been staff changes. It was nine years since I had been in the place but the furniture was the same, as were the bed covers and curtains. The carpet was still stained; the day-room still smelled of stale cigarette smoke. The only real difference was that this time there was purpose in my stay, and they had no control over how long I was there. It was entirely up to me. They still took my clothes away, however, which made me very aggressive. They searched through my things, made me have a bath with the door open, and then weighed me. I weighed only seven-and-a-half stone.

As I lay on my bed I heard someone crying. A pretty fair-haired girl was sitting on her bed with her face in her hands. I went over and sat by her, not knowing quite what to do. Rather awkwardly I put my arm across her shoulders.

'What's your name?' I asked.

'Joy,' she replied.

I couldn't help laughing a bit—it wasn't the most appropriate name in the circumstances.

'I don't want to stay here. I can't,' she sobbed.

Joy had been a nurse and was addicted to the drug Largactil. We became very friendly, and if she had not been there at nights I seriously doubt that I would have got through my detoxification. The nights were always the worst and reminded me of some of the nights I had spent there previously, just walking around, only this time my legs hurt too much to walk. So Joy and I spent many hours in an upstairs room, listening to records.

By the end of the first week I was feeling really ill and quite weak. Half-way through the second week I could happily have left the hospital, but thoughts of going to court kept me there. Something else held me too, but I didn't then know what.

When the day came for me to go to court I felt so ill that a nurse had to support me. So, this was it. I stood in the dock. It was the first time I had stood there actually aware of my surroundings and of the people in the court-room looking at me. Previously I had always been too high on drugs really to notice. Now I didn't like myself very much. All the evidence was given. My record was read out. It sounded appalling, even to me. The magistrates eventually went out to decide what action to take. I had to stand up while they were passing sentence.

'We are fully aware that you are on a suspended prison sentence, and we want you to understand that if we chose to we could commit you to prison. However, in view of your efforts to change your life-style, and taking into consideration the letter from Miss Grandfield of the Coke Hole Trust, we are going to give you an absolute discharge, and the discharge comes with our very best wishes for your recovery and indeed for your future.'

I couldn't believe it! I looked at my solicitor, who winked at me. On the way back to the hospital I remembered what Joy had said as she hugged me before I left to go to court: 'I'll pray for you.' I went to find her and told her what happened. She was delighted for me. We didn't talk about what she had said about praying for me. I thought I'd rather forget it.

I really don't know what kept me at the hospital for another week; maybe Joy had been praying again! I wasn't looking forward to going to Ashley Copse. I felt intimidated by the idea of sharing a house with six other girls and two house-parents.

An hour or so before Sue arrived to pick me up, Joy came to find me.

'I shall miss you,' she said. 'You've helped me a lot. I'd like you to take this.'

She handed me a package and asked me not to open it until I was on my way.

'Thanks,' I said, 'you've helped me a lot too, probably more than you know.'

Sue arrived with Sharon, one of the girls from the house. Joy waved as we went across the bridge, down the long corridor and out to Sue's car. As the car started I was reminded of the last time I had left that hospital. In some ways I felt equally apprehensive. I remembered the parcel that Joy had given me and opened it. It was a Bible. I felt a bit disappointed. Inside the cover she had written:

> To Carole,
> The Lord bless you and keep you;
> The Lord make his face shine upon you and be gracious
> unto you;
> The Lord turn his face towards you and give you peace.
> With love, Joy.
>
> *4 April 1983*

I put the Bible to one side, and tried to concentrate on where we were going.

8

Ashley Copse was a large, rambling house in the country with outhouses and a wooded copse at the end of the gardens. The outhouses were home to goats, chickens and bearded collie dogs. Also in the grounds were a large duck pond, various sheds and a couple of caravans. In summer the house was covered with honey suckle and wistaria. Five other girls were there at the same time as me—Susan, Laura, Sharon, Lisa and Ellen. There were two house-parents, along with several other staff members, and the idea was that we should live together as a family, sharing the chores as well as leisure time. As it was a large house with a big vegetable garden, there was always something to do. The house had to be cleaned, the chickens fed, the goats milked, the duck pond cleaned out, the lawns mowed, the fruit picked in the summer and bread and pies baked for the market.

For most of us it was a whole new experience. The discipline of getting out of bed, having breakfast cleared away and chores started by nine o'clock was about as much as I could cope with at the beginning. By the time the chores were finished at ten o'clock a.m. I was about ready for bed again!

My awareness of and sensitivity to the feelings of others in the house, including the staff—Judy, Clive and Cathy—was initially non-existent. Being at that time wholly concerned about myself, my attitude was one of lazy complacency. The staff were there for my benefit; they must be paid for what they did, so why should I care if I hurt them with thoughtless or even thought-out harsh words?

In fact, the staff were very poorly paid, though money was not a great consideration. They were there serving and loving us in the belief that they were doing exactly what God had told them to. All the staff were Christians, but there was no attempt on their part to force religion down our throats. There was an informal 'quiet time' two or three times a week, which we were welcome to attend—but none of us ever did! What got through to me was the love they showed in all they did. Their capacity to love was enormous, even in the face of verbal abuse and when it seemed to be just a waste of time.

During the first month or so at Ashley Copse I had to learn to face and cope with many different emotions that had been successfully suppressed for years.

Heroin has an anaesthetic effect as far as emotions are concerned. When this is removed, one experiences almost an eruption of emotion. Sometimes the pressure became too intense, and I felt a need to escape from myself, from all the things I could see and didn't like, feelings of hatred, bitterness and sometimes intense emotional pain. So after the first month I ran away and hitched a lift back to Bristol.

I remember very distinctly the first house I went to. I had been there hundreds of times before, but even as I rang the bell I sensed that this was going to be different. It seemed strange that I had never noticed on previous visits how squalid that room was. There were six or seven other people sitting around, most of them in the process of having a fix. I held the syringe in my hand and involuntarily shuddered at what I was about to do. I felt curiously detached, and set apart from these people and their life-style, which had once been mine. I had my fix and felt nothing. There was no great buzz, the intensity of emotional pain was still there, and I hated myself more than I thought possible.

For two weeks I tried to fit back into my old life-style. The amount of heroin necessary to numb my emotions would have killed me. At the end of those two weeks I phoned Judy and asked if I could go back to the Copse; I had to go on. They came all the way to Bristol to pick me up, and when we got back people were actually pleased to see me after all the worry I had put them through. I hadn't given them a second thought while I was away.

As time went on I began to see clearly the beauty of God's creation: flowers, trees, the sun, the moon and stars were all things I had never really noticed before. I hadn't noticed the way the leaves rustled a kind of music when the wind blew, or the way the birds sang at the crack of dawn.

Harry Coad phoned me occasionally, and one evening he told me that there were over two hundred people in Bristol praying for me. How angry that made me! I couldn't understand why people I had never met should want to pray for me, particularly since they prayed to a God I didn't believe in. Harry used to send me Christian testimony books. These aroused mixed feelings. I didn't want to appear too interested in them in front of the other girls, so I read them when I was alone, usually at night.

One such book was Rita Nightingale's *Freed for Life*, in which Rita told the story of how she had been imprisoned in a gaol in Thailand, and how she eventually became a Christian. I couldn't put it down. The part that affected me most was when she explained how, after she became a Christian, her attitudes changed and she began to relate to other people in prison.

After reading this book I started asking questions about this God. Why should God forgive me? Hadn't I done too many wrong things? Wasn't it too late? Jesus came across particularly powerfully through the book, and looking back I suppose I was challenged, but my attitude was, 'Well, who is this Jesus guy anyway?' and I tried hard to dismiss him.

There were also amusing moments at Ashley Copse. One hot, sticky summer bank holiday, Laura and I were bored and irritable. We needed somehow to release our pent-up emotions and have a laugh in the process. One particular member of staff, Cathy, used to take a lot of stick from most of us. We sent Ellen off to find Cathy, and bring her into the garden. Laura armed herself with the hose-pipe and hid behind a huge bush, while I climbed on to the roof of the shed with a large bucket full of smelly green duck-pond water. As Cathy approached, Laura jumped out from behind the bush and drenched her in icy cold water. At the same time the duck-pond water hit its target, covering her from head to foot in awful-smelling slime. If that had been Laura or me, I'm sure we would have come out with all sorts of expletives and avenged ourselves into the bargain. But not Cathy. She looked up. 'You cows,' she said, and burst into uncontrollable laughter.

Whenever one of the staff or one of the residents who had completed their rehabilitation was leaving, there would be a leaving party. We would spend several days making all sorts of amazing things—quiches, salads, pies, gateaux, fresh cream and strawberry meringues, chocolate mousse and a host of other delicious things. Some of us had a way of making sure we had the cake we wanted—we were just like little kids! Before anyone arrived and while nobody was looking, we would hide some meringues in places where nobody would find them, and eat them later. I remember opening a drawer quite a long time after one such party and finding what can only be described as a green furry ex-meringue filled with now not-so-fresh cream, and strawberries growing up the side of the drawer!

As the time approached for the guests to arrive we would all gather on the landing and peer through the curtains, just like nervous little girls at our first party. Nobody wanted to go down first. When we did eventually venture down some of us would hide immediately in obscure places, or casually find our way into the garden, breathing a sigh of relief as we lit our cigarettes, hoping that none of the guests would approach us wanting to have a polite chat.

Although most of us were in our mid-twenties, emotionally we were still just adolescents; when we had started using hard drugs our emotional growth had slowed down. So for me it was like having to grow up from the age of sixteen.

On one occasion one of the baby doves was very ill, and everyone said it was going to die. I doggedly refused to believe it and that night made up a bed in the sitting-room, with the intention of nursing the bird back to health. The alarm clock went off every three hours or so throughout the night, and each time I would try to feed the dove with warm milk through an ear-dropper. Once or twice I placed it under ultraviolet light for a short time. By morning it seemed to have recovered slightly, but it was a brief respite and the bird died later that day. I was devastated. Looking back now I can see that my reactions were like those of a child.

After three months restrictions on me were lifted, which meant that I could go for walks outside the grounds by myself, although I had to keep to the surrounding village. I used to take Mouse, one of the dogs, for a walk through some woods not far from the Copse.

While I was on one of these walks with Angie (a staff member from the men's house owned by the Coke Hole Trust) we reached a crossroads in the woods. We sat in the middle surrounded by trees and glorious sunshine. I asked Angie how she had become a Christian, but I didn't hear what she was saying; all my attention was taken by the radiant glow on her face, and the way her eyes shone as she talked. She was so peaceful, and seemed fulfilled. I wanted what she had.

Several days later Judy prayed with me. She had explained to me about Jesus dying for me on the cross. I felt pretty stupid and self-conscious, but if Jesus could change me into a new person it was worth feeling stupid, so I asked Jesus to forgive me and to come into my life and help me. Afterwards I was elated and on the best drug-free high I had ever experienced. It made me want to tell everybody.

In the Bible Jesus said: 'I tell you the truth, no-one can see the kingdom of God unless he is born again.' Most of us are able to see the world around us, but there is also a spiritual kingdom ruled over by Jesus. However, we can't see it unless we are born spiritually. Jesus explained that we each need to receive his Spirit into ourselves and be born again. I had shut him out all my life. His love, shown to me by Christians, had broken down much of my resistance and I knew that he loved me and that he died for me. He says to each of us, 'Here I am! I stand at the door and knock. If anyone hears my voice and opens the door, I will come in.' At last I was prepared to open the door a little.

During my time at Ashley Copse I had regular contact with a solicitor in Bristol in connection with my daughter Joni, who had been taken into care when she was nine months old. I tried repeatedly to get her back, visiting her on several occasions. Now it appeared that her foster-parents wanted to adopt her. She was then two-and-a-half years old. I had been desperately trying not to think too much about the situation. I felt guilty because I had let her down. A very big part of me wanted her back, but I was terribly aware of the damage this could cause, since she would not know me and had come to know and love her foster-parents as her mummy and daddy. After a traumatic emotional struggle I came to the conclusion that if I truly loved my little girl then I would let her go.

The time between making the decision to have her

adopted and having to go to the magistrates' court to sign the papers seemed to pass too quickly. I felt that it had slipped through my hands. When Judy drove me to the court I couldn't speak. I sat in the car remembering Joni with her fair hair, bright blue eyes and cheeky smile. Then the picture changed. The last time I had seen her she must have been nearly two years old. She had screamed as I left and I had turned round to see her tiny little figure pressed against the frosted glass door. I shall never forget it.

That moment came back to me as I walked into the court. There were three men sitting at a long table, with some papers in front of them. Judy guided me to the table; I felt like a clockwork doll. The men didn't ask me to sit down, only to sign the papers. My throat constricted as I battled to beat down the raw emotion that threatened to erupt. I signed the papers, and that was it. The whole procedure was indescribably cold. My mind went numb. Judy took me for a drive, which I remember very little about. Then she drove us back to the Copse.

In the relatively short space of time since becoming a Christian, I had become aware of the awful damage I had done to my children, particularly Joni. I lost sight of God and Jesus in the situation, not knowing how to say 'Help me', or not feeling able to say it, and certainly not realising that God was even more concerned for my children than I was. All positive thought about myself and life in general diminished. In a way I suppose a part of me blamed God.

I was in such turmoil about it all that within a few days of signing the adoption papers, I ran away and hitched a lift with the first car that stopped. It didn't matter where it was going. It happened to be Newbury. My memory of exactly what happened is pretty vague, but I overdosed and found myself in St John's Church. All I remember is the vicar placing his hands on my head and praying continuously until the ambulance arrived. I was in hospital for a week with a bad liver, and so had time in which to reflect.

Even with this time, though, I still felt angry and confused, so when I returned to Ashley Copse for the third time, I went out of my way to destroy relationships that had been built up, wanting to hurt everybody, myself most of all. I succeeded in doing just that, and when I chose to leave Ashley Copse for the last time it was under a cloud. There was no way I would be able to go back.

At this stage I had no real sense of the selflessness of the Christian life or of the cost of being a disciple of Jesus. I had prayed and asked for forgiveness. I had asked Jesus to come into my life and make me a new person, but that was as far as my commitment went. I thought that it would all just happen, and I didn't really have any idea of what I was supposed to do or how I was supposed to grow in the faith. The Christian love of the staff had broken down a lot of barriers, but there was so much that I didn't understand.

At Ashley Copse Judy had once read me a psalm, which I later memorised—Psalm 139. It was always at the back of my mind:

> You hem me in—behind and before;
>   you have laid your hand upon me.
> Such knowledge is too wonderful for me,
>   too lofty for me to attain.
> Where can I go from your Spirit?

Where can I flee from your presence?
If I go up to the heavens, you are there,
  if I make my bed in the depths,
  you are there.
If I rise on the wings of the dawn,
  if I settle on the far side of the sea,
  even there your hand will guide me,
  your right hand will hold me fast.
If I say, 'Surely the darkness will hide me
  and the light become night around me,'
  even the darkness will not be dark to you;
  the night will shine like the day,
  for darkness is as light to you.'

9

After leaving Ashley Copse I went back to Bristol yet again. For two weeks I had the most dreadful sense of not belonging anywhere or to anyone. I knew that I could no longer fit back into the life-style I had had previously. I seemed to be caught between two worlds.

Sitting on the pavement outside a pub with my one plastic carrier-bag containing my few belongings, I watched the traffic streaming past, and yet I didn't see it. There must have been hundreds of people walking up and down the pavements; I gazed at them, yet to me they were faceless. I looked at the buildings on the opposite side of the street, and they all seemed to merge into a grey concrete mass. A few yards to my right was a drunk who didn't know whether he was going into or coming out of a bright red telephone-box. I looked away again. I felt like a nomad in some kind of concrete desert.

I was running away from God and yet I knew I had nowhere to run to. Some of the words of the psalm I had learnt came back to me now:

You perceive my thoughts from afar....

You are familiar with all my ways....
If I make my bed in the depths you are there....
Surely the darkness will hide me....
Your right hand will hold me fast.

I was very aware that God knew what I was doing and why I was doing it. I didn't then realise that when I had prayed and asked Jesus to come into my life, God's Spirit had entered into my heart, and that because of this nothing would ever be the same again. I still didn't really know how to call out to God, or maybe I just wasn't sure whether or not I would be rejected by him.

The drunk almost tripped over my foot, muttering, 'Gis ten pence, will ya luv. Aa need a drink.'

I gave him a couple of pence and he wandered off. I glanced at the phone-box again, thinking to myself that it was probably the brightest thing in the street. I wondered about phoning the Coke Hole Trust. What would they say? It was worth a try. Picking up my plastic bag, I went over to it. It stank. I dialled the number.

'Hello. Ashley Copse.'

'It's Carole.'

'Where are you?'

'Bristol. Can I come back?'

'No. Not this time. If you want to come back you'll have to come for another interview.'

'I don't know what to do,' I said miserably.

'We're sorry. We can't help you this time.'

I put the phone down and went back outside to sit on the pavement. The heaviness I had been feeling inside increased. I didn't want to be lost like this. What could I do? It was then that I remembered Harry Coad. I went back to the box. I felt more nervous about phoning Harry than I had about phoning Ashley Copse. Harry told me to stay where I was and said he and his wife, Mary, would come to pick me up. I was still sitting on the pavement when the car pulled up.

'Come on then,' Harry said, 'get in.'

I picked up my carrier-bag and got into the back seat. Harry introduced me to Mary. She looked very kind and spoke with a rather posh accent.

'We were just about to leave the house when you rang,' Harry said. 'We were on our way to a meeting. Now, I'll tell you what I'm prepared to do. I'll sort out a night's lodging for you on condition that you come to this meeting with us.'

'What meeting?' I asked.

'It's a church meeting, and there's someone I want you to meet who'll be there. His name is Roger Graham. I think you'll like listening to the woman who's going to be speaking. Her name is Rita Night-ingale.'

I was silent. Yes, of course! I recognised the name. Her book had made such an impression on me at Ashley Copse.

'Well,' he said, 'are you going to come or not?'

'All right.'

I don't think there was any more conversation until we stopped on a hill with a very high wall. On the other side of the wall, set right back from the road, was a row of tall houses, one of which was a bed and breakfast place. Harry booked me in and a woman showed me to my room. I left my carrier bag on the bed, locked the door, and we all went back out to the car.

'When did you last eat?' Harry asked.

'I can't remember.'

'Well, are you hungry?'

'Yes,' I said.

'OK—we'll stop somewhere on the way, and you can eat in the car.' We stopped outside a fried chicken take-away and Harry bought me several pieces of chicken and a huge portion of chips, with a canned drink. We arrived at the church just as I finished eating.

As we went in, Harry said, 'Stay there: I'm just going to see if I can find Roger.'

Rita Nightingale had already started speaking, and Mary said she thought we ought to sit down.

'In a minute,' I said, 'I've just got to have a cigarette. I'll be on the steps outside,' and with that I went quickly outside, sat on the bottom step and breathed a sigh of relief. I didn't want to sit in the church. I felt threatened. I sat on the steps for some time chain-smoking.

'Hello,' said a voice behind me. 'Mind if I join you?' I turned round to see a man brandishing a tobacco pouch.

'No,' I mumbled.

He sat down next to me and was quiet for a time, just smoking.

'My name's Roger Graham. Your name's Carole, isn't it? Harry has told me about you.'

'Has he?' I said, looking straight ahead as I smoked.

He told me a little about himself. He said that he used to be an addict but that he now worked for the Prison Christian Fellowship. He was a friendly chap, quite short, and slightly balding. I sensed after a little further general conversation that he was genuine, and probably knew where I was at.

'Look,' he said, 'do you want me to help you?'

I nodded.

'Well, I can't talk to you properly here. I'm staying in Bristol overnight. I could come and see you in the morning. What about that?'

'OK,' I said.

Harry and Mary were coming out of the meeting, and they talked for a while with Roger before we went back to the car.

'Roger's told me he's seeing you tomorrow. He'll pick you up and bring you to our home, and then you can stay with Mary for the rest of the day,' Harry said.

We were about to drive past the fried chicken take-away again.

'Are you still hungry?' asked Mary. 'Have you had enough to eat?'

'I am a bit hungry,' I said.

Harry went off and bought me another load of chicken and chips, then dropped me off at the bed and breakfast place.

When I woke the following morning and remembered that Roger was coming, I felt terribly nervous about it. I waited. There was a knock on the door.

'Come in,' I said, 'it's not locked.'

We talked for a short while about several things. First Roger talked about how I needed to receive healing for the hurt my dad had caused me when I was a child, not so much the physical hurt, but the emotional damage that had been done. Then he explained that becoming a Christian was just a first step and I needed to be filled with the Holy Spirit. I understood some of the things he said but by no means all of them.

Roger took me in his car to Harry and Mary's house.

I remember thinking how beautiful it was, and what an absolute contrast to all that I was used to. Everything was clean and smelt fresh—at least it did until Roger and I lit up our cigarettes. There were many beautiful pieces of furniture and ornaments. First we had coffee, and then Mary took us into her living-room. She and Roger started talking to me about how I needed to be baptised in the Holy Spirit. They explained that to be baptised meant to be completely immersed; I needed to be completely immersed in God's Spirit and in his love.

'Do you want us to pray for you now?' Roger asked.

'Yes,' I said.

I knelt on the floor while Roger and Mary prayed for me. They prayed that God would heal the hurt that my father had caused. As they started to pray, I felt an inward struggle going on. A part of me didn't want to let go of the hurt that I had carried with me for such a long time. I was afraid as well of what would happen if I did let go. But Roger and Mary kept on praying, and gradually, little by little, I started to let go. I realised my face was wet with tears. I couldn't stop weeping, and as I wept Roger and Mary prayed that I would be totally immersed in God's Spirit and surrounded by his love. I began to feel an incredible warmth welling up inside me, filling the empty space that was left from my hurt; I was overwhelmed with God's love for me, so much that I cried again, only this time with tears of joy.

They both held on to me for a long time. When the praying stopped I didn't want to move. For the first time in my life I felt beautiful inside, and I knew that I belonged to somebody. But more than that, I knew myself to be loved—absolutely and unconditionally.

Some time later Roger started telling me about his

wife, Janet, and their children, Elizabeth and Lydia. Before he left he said that if the Coke Hole Trust would not have me back then I was to let him know.

For the two days that followed Mary took me under her wing. She talked to me, listened to me, fed me, washed my extremely grotty clothes and generally gave herself to me. Our backgrounds were worlds apart, and yet I knew that she loved me. During those two days I also went for another interview at Ashley Copse, sensing that it would be pointless. It was. I must say here, however, that they were absolutely right to turn me down; it was a form of discipline for me.

I phoned the number that Roger had given me. A woman answered.

'Hello,' I said, 'you must be Janet,' and went on to explain who I was and why I was phoning. I was invited to go to Newton Poppleford, a village in Devon, to stay with Roger, Janet and their children. Roger picked me up at Exeter Station. I didn't know what it was going to be like living as a member of their family. Neither did I know how long I would last, but I meant to give it a really good try. I seemed to have a lot more determination somehow, and a desire to achieve something with what was left of my life.

It was dark when we pulled into the tiny drive of a little pink cottage. I don't know what had given me the impression that Roger and Janet were likely to have a big house. I suppose it must have been partly the fact that they had children and had asked me to stay as well. In fact, their house had just two bedrooms and a bathroom, two small downstairs rooms and a kitchen. As we went in, my first impression was one of warmth. When I entered the living-room Janet came out of the kitchen.

She had rosy cheeks, long fair hair and sparkling blue eyes. After hugging me she made me a cup of tea, which I promptly spilt on the carpet, partly through nervousness. Elizabeth and Lydia came and sat next to me. They were pretty children. Lizzie, the elder, gave me her hairbrush and asked me if I would like to brush her hair. As I did so I felt very emotional. I didn't know how well I was going to cope with living with these two little girls. They brought to mind my own children, and those memories were still very painful.

For a week or so I slept on the floor downstairs. My alarm clock in the mornings was Lizzie and Lydia sitting on me!

During that first week I met Julie. She had been an addict in London and came from the East End. We became quite close. She lived in a caravan about a mile from Roger and Janet's house, and it was through her that I managed to rent a caravan from her landlord. Roger had to knock the wall down to accommodate the little caravan in their parking space, and it was with a sense of excitement that I moved in.

In many ways it was good for me to stay close to the family, and yet have a measure of independence. I still needed a lot of support. I spent many hours shut away in the caravan listening to Christian teaching tapes and reading through piles of study books on the Bible. It seemed that I couldn't get enough of it. I had a real hunger to learn more about Jesus. I became quite close to Janet and the children, and was able to talk to her a little about one of my children. However, there was a constant temptation to drink since I was opposite a pub. I did go in a few times but didn't stay for very long.

I spent a lot of time with Julie too. Through listening to her talking about her baptism I decided to ask Roger if I could be baptised by immersion. I had been christened as a child, but it held no significance for me whatsoever. In the Bible people were baptised in water after they had believed in Jesus and decided to follow him. Going under the water is like having our old life buried so that we can come out again into a new life. I felt that this was the next step for me. I wanted to make a public declaration that I was a Christian and that Jesus was Lord of my life. I phoned Harry and asked him if he would help Roger to baptise me and he agreed gladly. I had very mixed feelings about it. I couldn't swim, and was terrified of being under water, but I knew I had to do it.

So on 26 November 1983 I was baptised in a swimming-pool belonging to a conference centre. There was a small Christian convention going on, so the building was being used by other people. I had borrowed a white skirt and blouse from Janet to be baptised in. As I walked through the door of the swimming-pool with Julie I was shocked to see that there were a lot of people actually in the pool! Roger, Janet, Harry and everybody else were standing in a corner, waiting for us.

Julie burst out laughing, 'Oh no,' she said, in her broadest cockney, 'now what are we going to do?'

Roger was very cool and collected about it and took it all in his stride. He calmly announced, 'Excuse me, everybody, excuse me—we're going to have a baptism now, so could everybody please be quiet for a few minutes.'

Some people got out of the water and sat on the side of the pool and others just stood where they were. I felt a knot of nervousness in my stomach. Julie was grinning at me, and I suddenly giggled. I waded into the swimming-pool to stand between Roger and Harry. They held me from behind. By this time my heart was thumping rather dramatically and I remember praying that I wouldn't panic while I was under the water and kick my legs! Roger asked me a question about my faith in Jesus. I answered. Then I was lowered into the water. For some reason I had my eyes open, and I saw the water closing over me from either side of my body. It really seemed as if I were being buried, and when I came up out of the water I felt more alive—and very grateful not to have kicked anybody!

Everybody was singing, 'Jesus, take me as I am, I can come no other way. Take me deeper into you, make my flesh life melt away ...'

Then everyone was praying for me. Roger read something from the Bible: 'You shall be a crown of beauty in the hand of the Lord and a royal diadem in the hand of your God.'

What a promise to me, and I hadn't done a thing to deserve it!

One of the things I struggled a lot with at first was money. I had absolutely no sense of value at all. I might have thirty pounds one day and the next day it would be completely gone on totally unnecessary things. I simply had no control as far as money was concerned. One day Roger got tired of me asking him to lend me money and suggested that I gave him a certain amount of my Social Security money each week to keep for me. It really was a case of if I had it I spent it. It was a long time before I could go into Exeter with ten pounds in my pocket and come back with more than five pounds.

Another thing I struggled with was a need to talk to somebody about my various occult experiences. I knew that it needed to be sorted out, but something stopped me from mentioning it. There had been a period in my life when I became more than a little interested in ouija-boards, to the extent that I was instrumental in introducing others to it. Also, for a period of several years I had occasionally told fortunes with tarot cards, and I attended several seances.

The people who used ouija-boards weren't all people from disadvantaged backgrounds. Some of them had the most stable of homes. People who had their fortunes told with the tarot cards and others who did the readings were not necessarily into drugs; in fact, some held down steady jobs and several were married with children. So a deprived background cannot be blamed for anybody's involvement in the occult, or indeed involvement with drugs, although there are cases where involvement with drugs and the occult go hand in hand.

Everything I have done in my life I have chosen to do, whether consciously or subconsciously. It was therefore important for me to acknowledge personal responsibility for these things. The battle raged within me, and it was Julie, having had similar experiences herself, who recognised that something was happening to me.

For an hour or so Roger and Julie sat with me in my caravan, praying about each year of my life, including my childhood and teenage years. They spent some time praying about the areas of my life where I might have been involved with the occult but couldn't remember.

(There had been many times when I had woken up in the mornings not knowing where I had been or what I had done, so it was vital that those areas of my life were covered.) As they were praying for later years I started to feel really tense inside, sensing an almost physical struggle going on within me. This struggle seemed to go on for a long time, although in reality it can't have done.

At the end I vomited. Then I was laughing, a joyful laugh, because I knew that the battle had been won. I felt a tremendous sense of having been set free from things that had bound me for years. We went into Roger's house and he made me write down every person I could remember who had used a ouija-board with me, and people I could remember reading the tarot cards for. After that we all prayed for each person on the list and spent some time praying for those whose names I couldn't remember. Then Roger burnt the list in the fire, and I knew peace in my heart once again.

Shortly after this I decided one day to walk into Sidmouth, a few miles away. I wanted to see the sea. It was further than I had thought, but I eventually got there. There is something very special and healing about being surrounded by one of the most beautiful parts of God's creation. It was the middle of December, and there were very few people about. I stood on the sea front, watching those great crashing grey waves, the spray sprinkling my face. My lips tasted of salt, and the air was sharp and fresh. It was there that I suddenly learned how to talk to God in a real way. I talked to him much as I am writing this down. I already knew that Jesus was my Saviour and Deliverer but I learnt that he is also my friend. The thought made me laugh aloud because of the realisation that I knew this person who was bigger and better than anything and everything, and yet who wanted to be my friend. I thought it was just amazing.

Since leaving home I had always hated Christmas, and associated it with negative events in my life, like being told that I couldn't have Joni back. Roger, Janet and the children were going to Plymouth for a few days and weren't happy about me being by myself. I insisted that I would be OK. I wouldn't have been all right if there had been a lot of people around, so they agreed to let me stay in the house by myself.

I found it a very painful experience to watch this family, whom I had grown very close to, preparing for Christmas. The girls were so excited. The decorations were up, there was a Christmas tree with fairy lights and more cards than I had ever seen before in one house. I walked around with an ominous lump lodged in my throat.

After they had gone I sat down in the living-room by the fire, trying to watch the television and smoking. It was only another two hours until midnight communion in the parish church up the road. I decided I would go and went for a walk first, to kill a bit of time. Eventually I heard the church bells, and made my way there. I sat down amongst quite a few other people. Many of them had come straight from the pub next door and some of them were drunk. I just didn't feel right sitting there, and had an overwhelming desire to get out. I stood up when everybody else did and left while they were singing. I walked back to the house and sat in the dark for a long time, with just the Christmas tree lights and the glow from the embers in the fire.

I remembered Joni and that awful Christmas without her, when I had thrown the tree out of the window. The lump in my throat seemed to have got bigger. I sat in the armchair letting the tears run down my face unchecked and they seemed to flow for a long time before I finally broke down completely.

As I started to calm down I had the most beautiful experience. I felt as though I were being cuddled and I knew that God was comforting me and that he wanted to heal the pain I felt about Joni. I relaxed, and as I did so the thought came into my mind that God knew where she was and what was happening to her, and for the first time ever I knew a sense of real peace as far as Joni was concerned. I still feel sad sometimes, but I no longer feel guilty.

God had given me peace about Joni, but as far as Philip, Mark and Calandra were concerned, I had no idea that God, in his great love, would one day give me reassurance about them too.

10

I had now been with the Graham family for quite a while and felt it was time that I looked for a job. Considering my record, I thought my chances of being employed weren't very good at all. However, I applied for a job that was being advertised in the local paper— for a live-in waitress at a hotel in Sidmouth, right on the sea front. With full knowledge of my background the owners, who were Christians, decided to employ me.

I hadn't held down a job for eight years or so, and even then I had drifted from one thing to another. It was important for me to learn how to keep a job as well as how to cope with a routine.

I moved into a room in the hotel just before the 'season' started, so I was broken in very gently. Had I started working in the middle of the summer season I doubt very much if I would have coped with the pressure. I definitely didn't like being told what to do and how to do it—I wanted to do everything my own way, and figure it all out for myself! Getting up in the morning was one of the hardest things. I used to set the alarm for 7.15 and had to be downstairs in the kitchens by 7.30.

Just as I started working in the hotel, Roger opened a coffee bar in Sidmouth called 'The Haven', and between shifts I spent a lot of time there. The building was in a bad way at the beginning. Julie and I spent many hours painting it, and making it look 'respectable'. It operated under the umbrella of the YMCA but there was a difference in that, unlike many YMCAs, Sidmouth YMCA sought to make Jesus Christ known to others.

Gradually my involvement with 'The Haven' increased and I became the secretary, which basically meant doing a bit of everything: making coffee, typing, answering the telephone, talking to people about Jesus and listening to people. After a few months I started working in the coffee bar full time and Roger found some Christians to support me financially.

I felt very privileged to live in this lovely part of the country, and spent much of my free time sitting by the sea and walking along the cliffs. I felt so much closer to God at those times than I did if I went to church.

I hardly went to church at all in the whole of the time that I lived in Devon. When I did go, I felt very aware of myself; I didn't 'fit in' or feel comfortable. In some respects I suppose I didn't look particularly approachable. Outside work I still wore my old jeans and shirts and had my hair very long. I used to find it very difficult to answer questions if anybody did approach me. I remember one occasion when I went to church dressed in that way. At the end of the service someone came towards me. I think he was a churchwarden. I immediately went hot with nervousness and felt prickly all over.

'Hello,' he said. 'Nice to see you here.'

'Hello...Yes...,' I stammered, feeling rather stupid and inadequate.

'Where do you come from?' he asked.

'Umm...well...Bristol mostly,' I mumbled. 'What a stupid thing to say,' I thought to myself. 'Why can't you just answer the man and stop stuttering?'

He looked at me, oddly I thought, though I suppose it could have been my imagination.

'What did you do in Bristol?'

'Now what do I say?' I thought.

'I...um...I was...,' I managed to stutter. 'Well, go on,' my head told me, 'just say it.'

'I didn't do anything,' I said in a rush, 'I was a drug addict.'

'Oh!' he said, his face changing perceptibly; this time he was the one who stuttered. 'Um...yes...well, thank you for telling me...' He made his apologies and walked off. I'm afraid I used incidents like this as excuses not to go to church. I didn't think about it very clearly: after all, if I had been that man I certainly wouldn't have known what to say.

Some months later I went back to the same church. By that time I had had my hair cut short, and had acquired some nice clothes and a pair of high-heeled shoes, as well as a big floppy black hat with a huge plume of feathers. I strolled into the church with my Bible under my arm and my nose in the air, peering under the ridiculously protective brim of the floppy hat, hoping the same churchwarden would be there so that I could show him that I was 'respectable' after all.

Unfortunately, because I was concentrating on maintaining an air of disdain, I didn't look where I was going. My heel caught in the carpet and I stumbled. Somebody giggled and my hat fell even further over my eyes, for which I was grateful as it hid my furious blushes.

One day I was invited to a church just outside Bristol to 'give my testimony'—in other words, to tell people how I came to know Jesus. Roger was invited too. I was a bit dubious to start with, and very nervous for several weeks beforehand. Julie had been giving testimonies for some time and she always felt nervous, even ill, before doing it. Now I knew how she felt. To be honest, however, I think a sizeable part of me liked the idea of being the centre of attention, having lots of people listen to me and waiting for their reaction.

The day came. We arrived at the church about half an hour before the service was due to start, and were taken into a back room where we prayed together before returning to the main church. My tummy was churning. There were a lot of people and a small part of me wanted to run away. Eventually I stood up to speak. I was shaking throughout, and when I had finished there was silence. I sat down feeling a kind of emptiness. At the end of the service people began coming up to me, shaking my hand and saying how wonderful it was that I could stand up like that and talk about my life and becoming a Christian, and wasn't it great to see what God could do. That was the point at which my adrenalin started to flow. I felt rushes of pleasure and excitement. I was getting a real buzz out of this.

Just as we were about to leave something amazing happened. A woman walked towards me, holding out her hands. She took my hands in hers and there were tears in her eyes.

'My dear,' she said, 'you don't know me, do you? We only met once. My name is Sandra Masey and I work in adoption and fostering. It has been precious for me to hear your testimony today. I dealt with all your children and I have been praying for you for ten years.'

I felt very moved. Sandra told me that all my children were with a Christian family! I could hardly take it in. This was almost unbelievable—a wonderful miracle brought about by God alone. My children had been adopted at separate times over a period of about nine years, and now they were all together in his care. As Sandra and I hugged each other, I thought of that Christmas when I had sensed God assuring me about Joni. Now in his gracious love for me he had given me a similar assurance and peace about Philip, Mark and Calandra.

Looking back, that seems the only 'real' thing about giving my testimony for the first time. The experience had created many conflicts inside me, but before these could be resolved, Roger had the idea of doing a tour, using the music from a record he had made and Roger, Julie and my testimonies, together with an audio-visual presentation of the gospel.

He began to set the wheels in motion.

A few weeks later, I was in the office sorting out Roger's lack of a filing system, when a man walked in asking to see him. The visitor was tall and dark-haired with the most intensely blue eyes I had ever seen. His name was Mike Simpson and he came from Newbury, where he ran a YMCA of a similar nature to that in Sidmouth. After he and Roger had finished talking,

Mike and I spent some time discussing the possibility of having an outreach on the beach during the Sidmouth International Folk Festival. We made plans for him to bring a group of young people down from Newbury to join a team from Sidmouth.

After Mike had left to return to Newbury, I remember thinking how much I liked him, and that I was looking forward to working with him. So in August, after many organisational conversations over the phone, we had our joint week of outreach to the people of Sidmouth and thousands of visitors to International Folk week. It was a new experience for everyone and it seemed strange talking to people from the beach through a microphone; they listened but continued walking at the same time. During the week Mike and I found we worked together really well.

At the end of the week we decided to have a midnight barbecue for everyone before the people from Newbury went home. We lit a fire on the beach, talked and sang. It must have been two a.m. when all the kids drifted off. Mike and I sat next to each other on the pebbles. The tide had gone right out; the cloudless sky was speckled with stars, and a red moon shone down, reflected in the water. We felt totally at one with each other, God, and his creation. It was very romantic. Suddenly, further up the beach a saxophone began to play. We looked at each other in amazement and simultaneously burst out laughing. It was so corny—like something out of a movie. That was when we decided we would like to go out with each other. I felt quite shy and when Mike first kissed me I felt like a sixteen-year-old; it was lovely!

Two months later, at the beginning of November, Roger, Julie and I left Devon to start the tour. It was to include church services, women's groups, men's groups, youth groups and clubs, and school assemblies. We were to go to venues in the North of England and the Midlands, including Scunthorpe, Hull, Sheffield and Birmingham. I felt quite anxious about the whole thing. By that time I had given testimonies in several churches and each time had had that curiously empty feeling immediately afterwards, followed by a rush of excitement at the end of the service.

The tour was quite gruelling; some days we did two or even three meetings. Mike and I phoned each other often that week and I was grateful to know I could call him at any time.

One evening we had to take a service in a Pentecostal church in Scunthorpe. Julie and I had been asked to wear hats in the church, which was fair enough, the only problem being that we didn't have any! The woman we were staying with that night produced a pile of hats and I was kneeling on the floor trying them on in front of a mirror when the phone rang. It was Mike. I was in a bit of a state as we had to leave for the church in ten minutes. The Bible talks in places about women having their heads covered and learning in quietness and submission. I am afraid I had always been rebellious and definitely not submissive. It was amusing then for me to be kneeling on the floor and wearing a hat when Mike proposed to me over the phone—a picture of submission; nothing more I assure you.

'Hello Carole,' said Mike. 'I know you've got a meeting soon, but I missed your call last night and I just wanted you to know that I'll be praying for you tonight.'

I asked him the usual questions like, 'How are you?' and then suddenly he went quiet.

'What's the matter?' I asked.

'Oh…um…nothing…'

'Yes there is. I can tell. You've gone ever so quiet.'

'Mmm. I know. Will you marry me?'

'What?' I shrieked.

'I said, will you marry me? Look, phone me later after the meeting.'

'No,' I shouted, 'I mean yes! I mean no, I won't wait till after the meeting and yes, I will marry you!'

Mike laughed. 'Is everybody else in the room?'

'Yes,' I said. 'I'll phone you later. Are you serious?'

'Of course I'm serious. I wouldn't joke about something like that.'

'Oh. OK. I'll phone you later then. Bye.'

I put the phone down. Everyone was looking at me. Roger pointed at me and said, 'He's the one who's supposed to go down on his knees, not you!'

Everybody else hooted with laughter; there wasn't time for more conversation; we had to leave for the meeting.

All this testimony-giving was affecting me badly, but my pride wouldn't allow me to say no and stop. I had come to a point where every single time I did it I became even more empty. It was like unzipping my soul and saying, 'Here you are; isn't it a mess? But I'm different now. I've changed.'

Well, maybe I had changed, but my testimonies certainly hadn't. I was saying the same things now as I had that first time and it hurt to do it. It hurt more than I had at first realised. Sometimes I even felt ashamed after giving my testimony: 'I did this; I did that. I was like this; I was like that. This happened; that happened; I became a Christian.' And that was it.

I talked at length to Mike about this, and through our conversations I realised that I was still in a sense 'living in the past'. Every time I gave my testimony I felt as if I were living through it all again. I convinced myself that I was still basically the same as I had been before becoming a Christian. I thought I was no different. All I ever did was talk about my past experiences, sometimes quite graphically.

On the other hand, at the beginning anyway, a part of me liked being on a pedestal, which is where some Christians tended to put me. I lived for these experiences of pleasure and excitement at the end of a meeting, until in a sense it became rather like having a fix. Sometimes I felt physically sick for several days afterwards.

I believe this was all tied up with not belonging to a church. What I needed, and had in fact needed since becoming a Christian, was to be loved and cherished within a fellowship of Christians; to be allowed time and space for God to take me further along the road away from my past, rather than be placed on a pedestal and left facing down the road in the direction from which I had come. I was not in a position to be able to receive from the Lord through teaching, others praying for me, or in worship. I didn't even really know how to worship God.

I had been emptying myself but nothing was filling me. My heart knew that I had Jesus, but my mind was in confusion. I came across a verse in the Bible that says: 'Work out your salvation with fear and trembling.' Thinking back now I can laugh at the way I interpreted that verse. I started trying to 'work out' whether or not I was a Christian. How could I be if I wasn't basically any different? Again it was Mike who lovingly pointed me in the right direction. 'That's what I feel I'm doing,' I said to him. 'I feel as if I'm working out my salvation in my mind, with fear and trembling in case it's not real.'

'But Carole, you don't have to work it out in your mind. Salvation is already in you, since you asked Jesus into your life. Your part is to allow it to work its way through you.'

Some time after this, Mike came down to see me in Sidmouth. I had moved into my own flat and, apart from the spiritual struggles going on within, I felt reasonably settled. Shortly after arriving, Mike showed me my engagement ring, which had once belonged to his grandmother. It was a beautiful ring in the shape of a fan.

'I want you to have this ring,' Mike said, but there's a condition attached to my giving it to you.'

'A condition!' I exclaimed.

'Yes. I want you to give me your word that you will move to Newbury at the earliest opportunity.'

I couldn't believe it. At the time it seemed that Mike wanted to take away the only stable thing in my life— my home.

'I can't,' I said. 'This is my home. I like it. I don't know anybody in Newbury. Where would I live? No, I can't.'

'Look, Carole,' he said, 'if you love me, then you'll do it. I'm not being mean and nasty; I just want to do what's best for you. If you're going to be my fiancée then I will not have you exposed to a perpetual round of testimony-giving. Think about it,' he went on, standing up to leave. 'I'll be in the Balfour pub at 10.15 this evening. You can give me your answer then.'

He left. I just didn't know what to do. I smashed a cup or two and then I cried. I knew he was right. I left it till the very last minute before I went to the pub. I gave him my word that I would move and we were formally engaged that evening.

Two days later I had a phone call from Bristol, asking me to give a testimony at a Prison Christian Fellowship rally to be headed up by Chuck Colson. I explained that I wasn't sure and needed time to think and pray about it, but the following day they phoned again.

'OK,' I said, 'I'll do it.' But in my heart I felt really unhappy about it. I resolved that this would be the last testimony I would give.

Several weeks before the rally, I went to stay with a Christian friend in Bristol for the weekend. While window-shopping on my own I bumped into two people I had known previously, who dealt in drugs. They were amazed at how different I looked, and invited me for a drink. I accepted, thinking it would be a good opportunity to tell them about Jesus. I went into that situation totally ill-equipped to deal with it. Even if I had been spiritually stable at the time, I should never have laid myself open to temptation in that way. I ended up taking some heroin and was ill for two days.

In this somewhat precarious spiritual state, I went to Christchurch in Bristol to give my testimony. There were hundreds of people, a stage with banks of flowers, video-cameras ... One man was giving his testimony as Chuck Colson arrived. I was next. Mike was there and so were Roger, Janet, Julie, Harry and Mary. I felt dreadful. I walked on to the stage and 'did my thing'. That's the only way I can describe it. As I began, I had an overwhelming desire to tell everybody how I really felt, so I started off, 'Well, what is a Christian anyway?...' and trailed off. I started again and said all the usual things. When I had finished everyone applauded; I just wanted to crawl away into a corner somewhere.

Several days later, I went to the doctor, who prescribed some fairly strong tranquillisers, and I spent most of my time shut away in the flat. I felt so depressed that I just wanted to hide away from Christians, responsibilities and anything that might demand the slightest little bit of me. I felt I couldn't give any more. While I was in this state I sent a letter to Mike, telling him I thought we had made a mistake: 'I'm sorry,' I wrote, 'I'm just not sure of anything any more.' Having posted this, I retreated into my shell for several more days.

I have to say that throughout this time I was very aware that there was no way God was going to let me go. I knew he wanted me to give him my past—all of it—and I was afraid to, because I felt that if I did, I would have nothing left. I wouldn't be anybody, and what's more, I would be totally dependent on him.

Three days after sending the letter to Mike, I got one back. I was so angry: some of the things he had written were exactly the things I had been struggling with.

The same evening there was a storm raging outside. For a while I just sat listening to it. By this time I was even angrier, but with God now rather than with Mike.

I didn't stop to pick up a coat before rushing out into the storm, slamming the door behind me. I walked to the sea front and along the promenade in the dark; before long I was drenched to the skin. I wanted to scream and rage but couldn't. I started to climb the steps leading to the cliff path, and had to keep stopping to catch my breath on the path itself. My hair was so wet that it stuck to my head. Water was running down my face and dripping off my nose, and my feet kept slipping in the mud. Eventually I got to the top of the cliff and stood there defiantly, the rain still beating down and the wind roaring in my ears. I screamed at the top of my voice:

'OK, God! What do I have to do? Where do you want me? What do you want?' I fell on my knees exhausted. 'I'll do whatever you want. Anything.' I began to cry, the tears on my cheeks mingling with the rain. In the end I lay face down on the ground, totally humbled before God. I lay there for some time, and when I finally sat up, I felt more full of God's love than ever before, and more in love with him.

Two weeks later I moved to Newbury, to a bed-sit in the same street as Mike. Moving from Sidmouth did not prove as difficult as I had expected, although I missed Julie at first and phoned her frequently.

Mike went regularly to an Anglican church, and I started to go with him. I found it very difficult to get used to in some ways. Some groups of people in the church seemed very close and were very loving towards each other. Other groups had the appearance of being close to one another but in fact weren't. There were times when I felt very vulnerable and exposed during a service, and at these times I usually went outside and smoked a cigarette before going back in.

I also found it hard to trust people with anything of myself, but I learnt a valuable lesson about the Church early on. I had previously been very critical of churches and individuals within them. Even now there must be many things that some Christians don't like about me, and there are certainly things I don't like about other Christians, but I have learnt about the value God places on each one of us. I know that he values me, that I am his precious child, and I know that it is God's grace alone that changes me and others.

11

During our engagement, Mike and I saw each other nearly every day, so he saw me at my most dramatic, my most selfish and my least confident. I had initially been attracted to Mike because he was so gentle and calm, and he always related to me in a way that was the complete opposite of the kind of treatment I had received from men in the past. Yet, although I was very much in love with him, I had constant nagging doubts about his love for me. I had never before been close to, or even met, anyone so gentle and loving, and there was something within me that wanted to provoke him to anger, to test the extent of his love for me. I wanted to trust him but found that I couldn't.

All these feelings came out not only during our engagement, but also, and to a far greater extent, in our early marriage. I gradually realised how much former relationships with men, especially my father, were affecting my present relationship with Mike and indeed with God.

Since arriving in Newbury and becoming involved with a church, I had been to many prayer meetings. Every time somebody began a prayer with the word

'Father', I would feel angry and very aggressive. Unfortunately, or maybe fortunately, Mike often started his prayers in this way. Afterwards I would be quiet and very clearly 'uptight' inside. Eventually Mike asked me why I was so tense after we had prayed together or even after going to a prayer meeting.

'It's because people pray to … Father,' I replied angrily, finding it difficult even to say the word. I just could not relate to God as my Father. Part of me was jealous because others could address God in this way but part of me simply couldn't imagine myself ever talking to God and saying 'Father'.

Mike showed me that although the pain my father had caused me as a child had been healed by God, I was still angry with my dad and had never forgiven him for what he did to me. On top of that I felt guilty about still feeling angry about it all. I needed two things—to forgive my father, even though he had been dead for many years, and to have the guilt about the anger towards him taken away by God.

Once I had understood and accepted this, Mike prayed for me, with loving arms round me and I just melted inside and was able genuinely to forgive my father. It was like having a veil taken away: I could see all the things that had hurt my dad, and probably caused him to be aggressive. His mother had died when he was two and his father when he was ten. At the age of fourteen he had been in the army, knowing only discipline and no affection. Later he had lived with my mum, knowing for many years that he couldn't marry her. (Shortly after his death I had asked my mum how long they had been married; she explained that it had been only two years, as she had been married already and had two sons when she met my dad.) Suddenly I understood all these things very clearly and no longer hated him; instead I felt sad because I had never once told him that I loved him, for, despite everything, I had loved him.

In the Bible God says that he is 'a father to the fatherless' and that in him 'the fatherless find compassion'. As I read these verses I saw how dependable the love of God my Father is: my Father in heaven would never let me down, and he would always love me unconditionally. The first time I prayed 'Father ...' I cried tears of relief.

My love for Mike and his loving attitude towards me enabled me to feel reasonably safe with him. I was, however, still completely incapable of relating to men in general, particularly men in the 'caring professions'— social workers, doctors, probation officers. I just used to clam up; in fact I still do with doctors, even Christian ones.

It is particularly difficult for me to write down my feelings about Mike and our relationship. Squirrels bury their very best nuts, and occasionally dig one up to devour. I'm rather like a squirrel as far as Mike is concerned. My feelings for him are very precious, and I like to bury my treasures, and take them out now and again to gaze in wonder at them. I have wonderful memories of special times together during our engagement. Like the time when we dressed up in ridiculous clothes, went out into the snow and built a wonderful snowman right outside a children's home so they could enjoy it. We dressed him in bright red braces, a scarf and hat and christened him 'Abomin'. He was almost as big as I was.

Before we were married Mike and I worked together a great deal with local young people. I was invited to Newbury one weekend before moving there to help with an outreach to young people. God used me that weekend to reach several youngsters who became Christians. Tom was the last person I saw. His parents were Christians but he wasn't. It was late at night and we were ready to finish. I really wanted this young lad to know Jesus, so I set about persuading him. I don't think there was much of God in it, but I believe God allowed me to make a big mistake so that I might learn from it. Tom made a commitment, and I didn't see him again until after I had moved to Newbury. He turned up at the YMCA coffee bar one night and asked to speak to me. We went off into a little room for privacy, and there was a long silence before he said: 'I don't want to be a Christian any more. It isn't working out right for me.'

'Could you just explain a little more?' I asked him.

'Yes,' he replied. 'I've done everything I was supposed to do. I go to church, I go to house groups, I pray and read my Bible. Nothing's any different. You asked me that weekend what I had to lose by trying it, so I asked Jesus into my life, I've been prayed with several times since, and I've done all the things a Christian is supposed to do...'

'But you haven't said anything about giving yourself to others or loving others,' I pointed out. 'What about the cost of being a disciple of Jesus?'

'Well, what about it?' he responded. 'You never said anything to me about that.'

I was stunned. In my eagerness I had made it too easy for this young lad to become a Christian. I had not explained that following Jesus takes real commitment, and how that commitment needs to be expressed in constant giving, loving and serving; there's no room for fickleness or selfishness.

For a long time after that conversation with Tom I was devastated that he had decided to go his own way, and felt personally responsible for his decision. He is now a constant reminder to me of the need to be honest with people about the cost of discipleship. It is not easy, and is probably more difficult for young people than for anybody else; it takes guts to be a Christian today.

I believe some Christians make it too easy for people, as I did for Tom, and when they later discover the cost of following Jesus, they walk away. Before I became a Christian, someone asked me, 'What have you got to lose?'

I remember thinking at the time that I had nothing to lose—nothing materially speaking, and I certainly had no self-respect or anything like that. So, I reckoned, I had absolutely nothing to lose. I was so wrong! I had, in a sense, to lose *myself*—my selfishness, my self-interest, self-indulgence, self-sufficiency (for what it was worth), my pride, and so much more. I had to be prepared to give everything of myself to Christ. Jesus was always very clear about the cost of following him. He said, 'Any of you who does not give up everything he has, cannot be my disciple.'

Mike and I began to plan our wedding, fixing the date for 11 May 1985, and deciding whom to invite. I went through lots of funny little 'phases' before the wedding; only two people from my own family would be there—my mum and younger brother—and I kept worrying about this and letting myself feel inadequate because of it. Then I struggled with the idea of wearing white, partly because a well-meaning Christian friend had asked, 'Don't you think you should wear cream?'

That little remark set me wondering what everyone would think if I wore white, so I thought maybe I should wear ivory or something like that. However, Mike wanted me to wear white and was convinced that Jesus would want me to as well; he reminded me that the Bible says, 'If anyone is in Christ, he is a new creation; the old has gone; the new has come!' In God's sight I was pure and clean and it didn't matter what anyone else thought. I was thrilled to bits. I had never thought I would be able to marry in a church and in white. My mum made my dress, and Mike's parents bought me a going-away outfit.

Though Mike and I were both excited about the wedding, we did, like most couples I guess, have a few tussles in the time leading up to it—a combination of nerves and the realisation that we were about to commit ourselves to each other for the rest of our lives.

The vicar graciously allowed us to organise the whole service ourselves. We chose Christian songs and hymns with a special significance for us, and a Christian friend wrote a beautiful piece of music for me to walk down the aisle to. We decided we would both read a passage from the Bible and would sit facing each other rather than the altar. All in all, it was definitely not a run-of-the-mill service!

There were some lighter moments in the run-up to the big day: two nights before the wedding I was in my night-dress, seeing off a friend called Elaine. Somehow I managed to lock myself out of the house, and my landlord and landlady were out for the evening. We went round to the back of the house. Borrowing a cheque card from Elaine, I inserted it between the upper and lower parts of the window, and slid the latch across. I then made the mistake of pulling the top window down instead of the bottom one up—some burglar I'd make! Praying that no one would see my forced entry and phone the police, and with Elaine falling about laughing in the background, I hitched my night-dress up to my waist with as much dignity as I could muster, and set about climbing through the window. It can't have been a pretty sight.

The wedding-day arrived; I was so nervous myself that I must have got on everyone else's nerves. To my astonishment I learnt afterwards that Mike had spent the morning, as cool and composed as ever, writing an article for the local paper!

I was late, of course—by about ten minutes. Roger gave me away, and Elizabeth, Lydia and two other little girls were my bridesmaids, with Julie as matron of honour. I can find no words to describe adequately my feelings of elation, joy—and nervousness—as I walked down the aisle. I had eyes for nobody but Mike, and throughout the whole service it seemed as if the only people present were ourselves and Jesus, surrounded by beautiful music and praise to God. At least half the guests were non-Christians and I felt they must have been affected in some way by our Christian wedding.

Still nervous afterwards at the reception, I ate hardly anything. There seemed to be so many people there, many of whom I had never met before. At last Mike and I were almost alone, being driven to a hotel for the night before flying to a castle near Inverness for our honeymoon. I felt like a princess!

Just after we were married I became the project

director for Off the Record, a new counselling service for drug-related problems in the Newbury area. I was asked to put together a training course for people interested in the work, and I did so incorporating many other people.

There is a widespread belief amongst Christians that with things like drug counselling, the person who has experienced drug or alcohol addiction is always the best person to counsel and train others to do so. My own view is that someone with personal experience can be invaluable in training others, but the assumption that the ex-addict is in fact a better counsellor is not necessarily true; it certainly wasn't in my own case. The people who helped me most were Christians who hadn't had 'experiences'—people like Mike, Clive, Judy and Mary. This is not to say that many other people didn't help me; they did. I just want to make the point that the person who's 'been there' doesn't necessarily make a better counsellor because of it. Someone looking at a situation from the outside can have valuable insights because they are relying on God for wisdom, not on their own knowledge based on their experience.

Many people from different churches came to the first training seminar. This number was halved by the second seminar, one of the reasons being that some felt we should be prepared to do more for addicts; they wanted us to have a doctor who would be willing to prescribe methadone linctus and tranquillisers. As I stated earlier, methadone is in itself so addictive that, in my view, prescribing this substitute drug for an addict is like handing a knife to someone intent on suicide. Every addict I've ever known would agree that the problem is not so much the drugs as what caused him or her to start taking drugs in the first place, so we aimed to concentrate on the person rather than the drugs.

Other people felt we shouldn't talk too much about Jesus in a counselling situation, but Jesus is the only answer for someone hooked on drugs, both to free him or her from the addiction and to deal with the root problem behind the addiction. In my view, not to talk about Jesus in such a situation would be like seeing somebody drowning and doing nothing to help.

We may have had a fairy-tale wedding and honeymoon, but the happy-ever-after bit didn't come quite so easily. Several months after Off the Record got off the ground, Mike and I started experiencing difficulties in our marriage. These difficulties were due mostly to my insecurity but also partly to the fact that we were both concentrating rather a lot on other people in our work. Mike's work with the YMCA was very absorbing and time-consuming and we were frequently not even at home at the same time.

I was very jealous and possessive of Mike. If we were walking down the street together and he so much as glanced at another female I would fly off the handle. I somehow got it into my head that he thought he'd made a mistake in marrying me. I was full of self-doubt and because of it I became very difficult to live with. One Sunday evening we had a row and Mike stormed out. He actually broke his umbrella after slamming it against a wall in frustration. This was my calm and gentle Mike, being reduced to a distinctly jumpy person because of having to deal with my fluctuating moods.

Eventually a Christian friend offered us the use of his

house near Bradford for however long we needed it. We took a week off and travelled up North by coach. This friend also paid for the tickets, because we were short of money. During that time we had many rows and many peaceful times, the latter mostly when we were walking across the moors. We had long discussions about our relationship and I know that by the time we left I was far more determined to give more of myself to Mike. I remember listening at that time to some words from a song by Don Francisco:

> Jesus didn't die for you because it was fun,
> He hung there for love because it had to be done...
> Love is not a feeling, it's an act of your will.

From that point I started to learn about what it means really to love, not just to be 'in love', which can be a very self-centred emotion. I learned that I should give willingly to Mike regardless of how I felt about it, emotionally or otherwise. Up to that point, if ever we had an argument about something, Mike was always the one to walk towards me, put his arms round me and say sorry, even when he was right and I was wrong. Now I knew that I could start being the one to cross the bridge between us and love him in the true sense of the word.

Something else I had done before we were married was to set up a prayer chain—a group of women from different churches who were prepared to pray in urgent situations at a moment's notice. The idea was that one person would phone two people and then those two people would phone two more people. There were twenty or so women on the chain altogether.

When we came back from Bradford we had a phone call from someone half-way down the chain.'

'Hello Mike,' she said. 'We've had a request put through the prayer chain.'

'Oh yes,' Mike said.

'Well, I just thought I ought to check it out before sending it any further down the chain.'

'Go on,' he said.

'The message was that Carole had left you and gone back to Bristol.'

Mike went berserk! We were both really angry. It may have been that the person who put the original request through had given a different message, and it had got distorted *en route*. But the point was that a valuable tool for God had apparently been used to convey unsubstantiated gossip. Sometimes we don't realise the damage we cause when we exaggerate. The experience certainly made Mike and me a lot less prone to exaggeration than before.

Of course, having said all that, there were many times when the prayer chain was very greatly used. I received a call one morning from a friend who has regular contact with the Coke Hole Trust. She told me that Susan, one of the girls I used to share a room with at Ashley Copse, had taken an overdose and was in a coma in hospital. I phoned the prayer chain and asked them to pray. Some weeks later she regained consciousness, but couldn't do anything for herself; she couldn't even speak. I phoned Susan's mother and asked if I could go to the hospital. She said yes but that Susan wouldn't recognise me. A week or so later a friend drove Mike and me to the hospital. Before we left I phoned the prayer chain and I remember asking them to pray very specifically that we would have an opportunity to talk to Susan on her own, that we would be able to pray with her and that, even if she couldn't recognise me, she would recognise Jesus and his love and forgiveness through our prayers.

Susan had become a Christian at Ashley Copse but things had gone wrong and she had tried to take her life. She had been such a vibrant person, full of life and energy. It was a shock to see her lying in her bed motionless, her lovely blue eyes staring at the wall opposite and her long fair hair splayed out across the pillow. Her mother left us on our own while she went to make a cup of tea. I took Susan's hand in mine and Mike held my other hand.

'Oh Susan,' I began, 'you know Jesus loves you and cares for you and he is so much bigger than we are and will forgive us anything.'

We started praying for her. We prayed that she would know the love of Jesus at that moment and that she would recognise Christ and the fact that he had forgiven her and wanted to fill her with his love. We stopped praying just a few seconds before her mother came back with the tea. I still held on to Susan's hand, praying for her in my mind. I had felt so sure that she would respond in some way. For a few moments I felt a terrible sadness inside, but then, as I watched her face, one solitary tear rolled slowly down her cheek and she bit her lip with emotion. I knew then that our prayers had been answered. Some weeks later my friend phoned to say that Susan had died in her sleep. I am absolutely certain that she is with Jesus.

Early in 1986 I discovered I was pregnant. Mike and I

were overjoyed. For me, it was a very special joy. Being pregnant brought all sorts of feelings to the surface. The very first thing that came into my mind was that God must love me very much. I had a few doubts about my ability to bring up a child, but those doubts didn't last for very long. I was no longer on my own. I had Mike and I had God.

My first appointment at the antenatal clinic was a little traumatic. The midwife asked lots of questions: 'Have you had a baby before?'... 'Where did you have them?'... 'Were there any problems?'... By the time she had written everything down I felt emotionally exhausted! She was a lovely lady though, and never seemed to doubt that I had changed. My one big fear had been precisely that. I had thought that 'they' might put our baby on the 'at risk' register or something, expecting them to have reservations, not believing that a person could be changed so much.

The first time the midwife came to the flat was during my paranoid phase. I gave it a really good clean before she arrived, thinking that she would be looking for signs of uncleanliness amongst other things.

When I was around five months pregnant my doctor sent me to the hospital for a scan. Mike came with me. The woman who was doing the scan suddenly smiled.

'Well,' she said, 'it looks as if you're going to have twins!'

12

I closed my eyes, my mind going back to the last time
somebody had told me I was going to have twins. I felt
Mike's hand on my shoulder, opened my eyes and
looked at his face. He was grinning and his eyes were
twinkling. I laughed. I couldn't believe this.

'Are you sure?' I asked.

'Oh yes,' the doctor said. 'Do you want me to see if I
can tell you the sex?'

We said yes and she told us that we were definitely
going to have a boy, but that she couldn't be sure about
the other one. I don't think it really sank in properly
until we were outside the hospital gates. Mike was
speechless. We hugged each other and virtually ran,
laughing, all the way down the hill.

I know that God is all-powerful and that there were
many ways in which he could have started a healing
process for my painful loss of Philip and Mark, as well
as of my little girls. But this! I was and still remain
completely overwhelmed at the incredibly loving way in
which God is healing me.

I thought back to twelve years previously and
remembered how I had felt then; alone and lonely,

scared and desperate, angry and very apprehensive. Now, by contrast, I was surrounded by love and never lonely; excited and making plans; joyful and only a little apprehensive. This was, for me, yet another new beginning. I remembered a verse from the Bible that somebody had given to me on a slip of paper after a meeting at which I had been speaking. It said, 'I will restore to you the years which the locust has eaten.' At the time, I had thought it a peculiar verse and hadn't understood what it meant. Now I realised that God had promised to restore all those wasted and painful years. He had been doing it since I had first given my life to Jesus, but it was only now that I recognised it.

In July when I was six months pregnant I resigned from Off the Record. I needed to stop but agreed to be available in an advisory capacity. Quite apart from anything else, I was so big it was becoming increasingly difficult to get around.

We had moved to another flat some months previously and were concentrating on decorating the twins' room. I had a very joyful pregnancy apart from the two months or so that it took me to stop smoking. During the first month I hid a packet of cigarettes in a saucepan so that Mike couldn't find them and every now and again, when I felt really desperate, I would wait for Mike to go out before dashing into the garden, hiding behind a bush in case he came back unexpectedly, and smoking a cigarette in record time. There were several times when he did in fact come back really quickly; this would necessitate my rushing back indoors and spraying everywhere with air freshener, before locking myself in the bathroom while I cleaned my teeth in case Mike wanted a kiss!

Apart from this I was mostly fine. I was able to wait patiently for the twins' arrival, even during the last month, though, like many pregnant women, I had occasional cravings for particular foods; God took care of this too.

One night at around eleven o'clock I had a real craving for something sweet. There was hardly anything in the food cupboard and we had no cash. Even if we had, we would not have been able to buy anything at that hour. Cuddling my lump, I waddled through to the twins' room where Mike was decorating.

'I can't stand it,' I said to him, 'I've got to have something sweet. I don't know what to do. Shall I phone Elaine?'

'Don't be daft,' Mike said, laughing. 'It's eleven o'clock! If we go to bed you'll soon go to sleep. In the morning I'll get some cash from the bank...'

'I won't be able to sleep,' I assured him and waddled back into the kitchen to rummage through the oddments in the cupboard once again. In the end I resorted to licking my finger and dipping it in the sugar bowl! Mike went to put the milk bottles out. There was quiet for a moment and then I heard him laughing. I went through to the hall.

'What's so funny?' I asked, licking my sticky finger.

He held out a plastic container. 'This is,' he said.

I took it, wondering what on earth there could possibly be to find amusing in a plastic container. I lifted the lid and my mouth immediately watered. Inside was a wonderful selection of little cakes.

'Where did you get this?'

'It was on the doorstep.'

I too burst out laughing then.

We were in church one Sunday evening in the middle of October. The service had finished and I was standing at the back of the church with several others, who were all asking the usual questions like, 'How long is it now?' and, 'Do you want boys or girls?' Suddenly I felt really peculiar and then my waters broke—right there in church in front of everybody! I stood there for a moment slightly shocked and half-heartedly prayed that nobody would notice. Fat chance there was of that!

'Mike,' I hissed. He didn't hear me.

'Mike,' I said a little louder. He still didn't respond.

'*Mike*,' I shouted.

'What?' he said, turning his attention to me at last.

'I think my waters have broken.'

He looked at the floor with his mouth open. So did everybody else. They looked like a load of goldfish.

'Oh, good grief!' he said.

We left the vicar's wife mopping up and went to get in the car. I felt very calm. I was more worried about how I was ever going to live it down. We drove home to pick up my case and one or two other things. I filled a flask for Mike and we made several phone calls before driving to the hospital. By that time I don't know who was the more jittery, Mike or myself. He was really tickled by the fact that my waters had broken in church.

My labour lasted six hours, during which time Mike sat reading a series of newspapers. Some things never change! I had been praying very hard that we would have a little girl and was convinced that we would. We had already chosen names for the twins. We'd decided to call our little boy Luke and if we had a little girl we planned to call her Charis.

I felt very peaceful while I was giving birth and was

aware that Mike was beside me the whole time praying. At 2.45 a.m. on 20 October 1986, I gave birth to Charis Mari. I looked at Mike with tears of joy streaming down my face and said, 'We've got a little girl.' There was no time to say more, because Luke Michael arrived exactly five minutes later.

Eventually the midwife, who was a Christian, left us on our own, knowing that we wanted to pray and thank God for Luke and Charis. As we held them in our arms we prayed that God would protect them and that one day they would know Jesus themselves. We had prayed for them from the time of conception right through my pregnancy. We did this believing with our whole being that life begins at conception. We were both so full of joy and thankfulness. I held one baby in each arm and thought how very beautiful they both were.

Mike left me at about 4.30 when I was taken to a ward with Luke and Charis. It was precious to have the twins with me all the time. The two evenings we all spent together in the hospital were very special. Mike drew the curtains round the bed and we sat together with Luke and Charis, completely overwhelmed by God's love for us.

After two days Mike came to take us home. We were inundated with cards, flowers and gifts. There were so many cards that we ran out of space and had to pin some on the walls. The living-room and our bedroom looked like a florist's and the stream of gifts for Luke and Charis seemed unending. I had never before felt so loved or cared for by other people. Up to that point I had known I wasn't alone because I had Jesus and I had Mike. But now I knew without a doubt that I had

been adopted into the biggest family imaginable—
God's family.

In the year that followed I gave myself up to the task
of looking after Luke and Charis. I spent a lot of time
laughing at their various antics and only a little time
crying when I got frustrated because I didn't know
what to do in certain situations. However, just after the
twins' first birthday, a bill went through Parliament
that was to be the means of God taking hold of my life
once more and giving me something new and specific to
do for him, something bigger than I could ever have
imagined.

In December 1987 I first became aware that David
Alton's abortion amendment bill was to go through
Parliament. The bill sought to reduce the time limit on
the availability of abortions from twenty-eight weeks to
eighteen weeks. I had for some time been very concerned about abortion in this country. Over the previous five years I had come across young women whose
circumstances were such that they were considering
having an abortion—women like Jan.

When I was living in Devon I had been asked to
write to a young woman called Jan who lived in
Sheffield. Just before we did our tour of the North of
England I received a letter from Jan telling me that she
was pregnant and didn't know what to do. She was
seriously considering having an abortion. Her home
situation was desperate. She lived with an alcoholic and
had three other children, all of whom were in temporary care. In her letter Jan said that she was confused,
had no one to talk to and was getting really desperate.

When we stopped in Sheffield on our way home I

went to find Jan. I knew at the time that there was very little I could do to help her except take her home with me for a holiday and spend some time just listening to her. She agreed to come back with me and stayed for four days. In the end she didn't have an abortion, not because of anything I said, but because she had been given time and space away from her home circumstances. She had been able to talk out all her feelings and had come to the conclusion that having an abortion would significantly worsen her situation.

At that time I had known very little about the methods of and reasons for abortion, and I only found out through my interest in David Alton's bill. I was so sickened by what I read and saw that I knew I couldn't just sit back and carry on with my life. I had to do something.

After discussion with Mike and some Christian friends I decided to draw up a petition in support of David Alton's bill and send it to church leaders across the country. The petitions were then sent back to me and I forwarded them, along with a letter, to various MPs. Even then I knew I had to do more.

One of the most widely-used arguments for abortion is that it is 'a woman's right to choose', but I believe that every woman should be made aware of exactly what she is choosing when she decides on abortion. One woman I counselled was still being affected by an abortion she had had fifteen years before.

I wrote a letter to the local newspaper on the subject of abortion and as a result a woman who worked with an anti-abortion group called LIFE phoned me up. Mike and I had a meeting with her after drawing up some ideas for setting up a separate, specifically Christian group in Newbury.

Christian Action For Unborn Life (CAFUL) was formed in February 1988 and became a Charitable Trust in early 1991. We knew that we had somehow to provide a very positive alternative for women with crisis pregnancies. In order to do this effectively we needed the support of the Church.

Our first aim was to educate the local Christian community about the means, effects and statistics of abortion, and we hoped that as a result this would inspire Christians to be prepared to care for these women, practically, emotionally, mentally and spiritually. We gave a total of eight presentations, incorporating drama, poetry, a video and a short talk. There was an extremely mixed response from churches, but, having done what we could to 'educate' the Christian public, our next objective was to provide a Christian alternative to abortion. We aimed to do this through providing a telephone help-line, effective Christian counselling and practical material help, which would eventually include a home run by CAFUL, where women could go for some months before and after giving birth to their children.

Despite the great reluctance of the majority of Christians to respond, we now have a dedicated group of people whose roles vary. Our team includes women who will act as befrienders, women to do child-minding, trained counsellors for crisis pregnancies and post-abortion counselling, male counsellors to counsel fathers, men and women who pray for the work, trustees, and people with secretarial and administrative skills. In 1989 our counsellors underwent an in-depth

148

training course, part of which was undertaken by the Firgrove Family Trust, who already ran a pregnancy counselling centre in Southampton.

Our vision for this work has broadened considerably. Centres for pregnancy counselling are springing up in the South of England and the Midlands but in the North there is as yet very little. We very much believe that the CAFUL Charitable Trust will be used to facilitate the setting up of centres in places of need. We may not run these centres directly ourselves, but we would aid Christian communities in those areas in the setting up of similar projects.

It is our earnest desire and prayer that through the work of CAFUL thousands of women will be made whole, as I have myself been made whole, and thousands of children's lives saved. No baby is unplanned or unwanted in God's eyes; David realised this when he wrote, again in Psalm 139:

> You knit me together in my mother's womb...
> My frame was not hidden from you...
> Your eyes saw my unformed body...

Author's Postscript

I began working with CAFUL at a time when I was being made whole and learning to be a mother myself. It was also at a time when reconciliation with my own mother was taking place.

After the wedding I maintained contact with my mum and she had been to stay with us for several weekends. It was quite strange at first having to get to know each other all over again. I didn't feel that I knew her at all and in the beginning our relationship was very tentative, on my part anyway. During one visit she read chapter eight of this book in its very early stages. Reading that, the incredible change she had seen in my life, and the way Mike and I related to each other affected her very much. That weekend she gave her life to Jesus and I felt so privileged to be there. Since that time our relationship has changed dramatically. At first it seemed very peculiar being able to talk to her freely about God, but then as time went on our relationship deepened. She was baptised in May 1989 with Mike assisting at her baptism. I found the whole experience extremely moving.

The situation with Mike's mum and dad was different. At first I had felt shy with them, not knowing what they would think of me. But they accepted me as a changed person, although it must have been difficult to understand, and probably still is, since they are not Christians. Mike's dad has been to me some of the things that my own dad was not, so my relationship with him has also been part of the healing process for me. I don't feel now that I have missed out as much as I once did and I am very fond of both him and Mike's mum.

In April 1989 we moved to another part of Newbury, this time to a three-bedroomed house, which we rented cheaply from Christians. Mike had become a district and county councillor and Luke and Charis were growing up into little people.

In the months following our move I kept coming across young women with crisis pregnancies. I was constantly reminded of the times that I had been in the same situation. I knew what it was like to feel that I had nobody to turn to, nobody to listen to me and hear what I was saying and, in the cases of Joni and Calandra, nobody to help me when I desperately needed it. It became obvious to us that we needed to get our tele-phone help-line off the ground as quickly as possible. We decided to call it Care in Crisis and I became the counselling director. The response has been very encouraging. We have a number of excellent links with people in the caring professions, several of whom are directly involved with CAFUL. Before long we expect to be receiving many referrals from GPs and others.

There are many truly amazing things about my life now. Firstly, there's Jesus, without whom my life would still be meaningless, empty and futile. And then Mike, whose love for me has broken down many barriers; without him I should feel only half a person. Of course there are Luke and Charis, our very precious children who were, and continue to be, a great inspiration to us in the work we are seeking to do for God. Then there is the wonderful knowledge that I belong to the biggest family in the world—God's.

Finally my work with Care in Crisis has given me the opportunity to reach out and offer help to women who find themselves in the crisis situation I myself was faced with three times.

God has taken hold of my life and transformed it. He loved me when I was at my lowest. He was always there, even in the very darkest of moments. He is there for you too, wherever you are and whatever your situation. Jesus said, 'I am the light of the world.' There is no darkness too great for him; in the words of Psalm 139:

> Even the darkness will not be dark to you;
> the night will shine like the day,
> for darkness is as light to you.

Publisher's Postscript

If you would like to contact Carole or give a gift or legacy to the Christian Action For Unborn Life Trust, you can write to:

> CAFUL
> PO Box 108
> NEWBURY
> Berkshire
> RG13 2HU

The Wounded: Part 1

by Bob & Barbara Hitching

The first in a series of books following the faith and fortunes of this unusual group of friends in the East End of London.

Share the agonies of life in the city with—

NICK, protector of the innocent and scourge of the guilty;

KENNY, his new Jewish friend and seeker after truth;

CHRISSY, Nick's beautiful sister and before long Kenny's girl;

ROULLA, who finds in Nick a willing convert to all things Greek;

HUSS, unwilling exile from his family and culture;

ANGIE, caught in a complex web of abuse and suffering;

RICK and SHEILA, whose home provides an oasis of security for Nick and his friends.

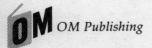 OM Publishing

The Wounded: Part 2

by Bob & Barbara Hitching

The second in a series of books following the faith and fortunes of an unusual group of friends in the East End of London.

Agonise with HUSS as he struggles with a heart-rending choice.

Weep with ANGIE as the wounds of the past continue to torture her.

Laugh with NICK and ROULLA as they chart the course of true love.

Follow too the paths of RICK and SHEILA, KENNY and CHRISSY as they and their friends grapple with the pressures of life in the inner city.

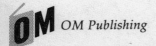 OM Publishing